ADVANCED LEVEL

Critical Reading for Proficiency 3

WITH OPEN-ENDED QUESTIONS

by
Stuart Margulies, Ph.D.
& Maria Goudiss

EDUCATIONAL DESIGN   *EDI 263*

ACKNOWLEDGMENTS

Excerpt from Maya Angelou's *Wouldn't Take Nothing for My Journey Now*, Random House, 1993.

Excerpt from Stephen Vincent Benét's "Lee."

Excerpt from Anne Frank's *The Diary of a Young Girl*, Doubleday, 1952.

Excerpt from Shirley Jackson's "Louisa, Please Come Home," from *Come Along with Me*, Viking 1968.

Excerpt from Franz Kafka's "The Metamorphosis," *Selected Short Stories of Franz Kafka*, Random House 1952.

Excerpt from Harper Lee's *To Kill a Mockingbird*, J. P. Lippincott (Harper & Row).

Excerpt from William Shakespeare's *The Tragedy of Romeo and Juliet*.

Excerpt from Edna St. Vincent Millay's "The Ballade of the Harp-Weaver."

Excerpt from William Saroyan's "The Broken Wheel," from *The Man with the Heart in the Highlands and Other Stories*, Dell 1968.

Excerpt from Mark Twain's "Edward Mills and George Benton."

Excerpt from John Greenleaf Whittier's "My Own Land Forever."

Carroll, Lewis, "The Walrus and the Carpenter."

Daudet, Alphonse, "The Last Lesson," The Frank A. Munsey Company.

Dickinson, Emily, "The Clouds."

Fields, Shelley, "A Double Life." Printed by permission of the author.

Gardner, Lewis, "Valentine." Reprinted by permission of the author.

Lowell, Amy, "Climbing."

Parker, Dorothy, "One Perfect Rose."

Rivera, Carmen, "Twilight." Printed by permission of the author.

Ruiz, Maribel, "Paradise." Printed by permission of the author.

Sadovnik, Lev, "Under the Hudson." Reprinted by permission of the author.

Taylor, Bayard, "A Night with a Wolf."

For information about permission, write to

Educational Design, 345 Hudson Street, New York, NY 10014-4502

ISBN # 0-87694-069-6   EDI 263

TABLE OF CONTENTS

PART 3: PRACTICE TESTS

INTRODUCTION TO THE STUDENT

The reading selections in this book will help you improve your ability to read critically.

Critical reading is the kind of reading you must do if you wish to fully understand a piece of writing. When you read critically, you make an effort to distinguish what is important from what is less important. You notice the order of events. You pay attention to cause and effect. You distinguish between fact and opinion. You make comparisons. In short, you don't just read words mechanically. You *think* about what you are reading.

In the selections in this book you will be asked to think about what you have read. As you go through the book, you will strengthen many useful thinking and reading skills. And, as an added bonus, you will improve your ability to do well on a variety of reading tests.

NOTICE: Photocopying any part of this book is forbidden by law.

5

PART 1

WRITING

1

STRATEGIES FOR ANSWERING OPEN-ENDED QUESTIONS

Most of the questions in reading tests are **multiple-choice**, so all you have to do is select one answer from three or four choices. But occasionally, you will be asked to respond to an **open-ended** question by writing a few sentences or even several paragraphs.

In this section you will learn some useful strategies for writing answers to open-ended questions. First read this article about Dean and Lorna.

EXAMPLE

Although Dean and Lorna had lived in Arizona for two years, they were still not used to life in the desert. They moved to Arizona from the East Coast because Dean suffered from allergies. The dry air made him feel much better. Still he and his wife missed the East.

"A house should have a lawn in front," Lorna complained. "Not sand and cactuses." Dean agreed with her. He thought that there should be trees all around and they should have leaves— leaves that were green in the summer, changed color in the autumn, and then fell off. "Trees should definitely be bare in the winter," he thought to himself. Most of all, though, Lorna and Dean missed the rain.

NOTICE: Photocopying any part of this book is forbidden by law.

It hardly ever seemed to rain in Arizona. At least, it didn't compare to what they were used to. When they lived near the ocean, there were sometimes weeks of rain. Dean loved to stand and watch the rain fall. Sometimes Dean and Lorna would go swimming in the rain. They loved water of all kinds. Now both Dean and Lorna felt dry all the time. They couldn't decide if they felt more like raisins or lizards. They decided to see what they could do to bring a little rain into their lives. Dean went online and did some research. He discovered a book about Spain and a palace which had a system of fountains and little streams which used recycled water. The water flowed and bubbled throughout the grounds of this palace. Then the water returned to where it started and started over.

This seemed like a wonderful idea to Dean, so he designed his own kind of fountain. He turned on the sprinkler and caught the water in a pool that he made out of clay. The water in the pool drained into a hose that went into the sprinkler. Every day that they could, Dean and Lorna would get in their swimsuits and play under the sprinkler in the pool. The recycled water felt like rain to them. They were happier than ever before.

To get a high score on an open-ended question, read the question carefully. Be sure that:

❖ you answer the question that is asked

❖ you answer all parts of the question

Be sure that you do NOT:

❖ limit your answer to a single word or phrase

ANSWERING THE QUESTION THAT IS ASKED

Suppose you were asked the following question:

1A. **How did Lorna and Dean feel about the desert? Support your answer with details from the passage.**

You might answer with a few words:

	They weren't used to it.	

This answer is incomplete: Lorna and Dean weren't used to the desert. But this answer doesn't include enough information. The question asks you to include supporting details from the passage. There is no way that a few words or a short sentence can earn top grades in open-ended questions on tests.

See how a student named Monica answered another question.

1B. **What did Dean and Lorna miss about the East Coast? Give details from the article to support your answer.**

Monica's answer:

	Dean and Lorna moved to Arizona because Dean had allergies. They
	were much better in Arizona because it was very dry. The desert
	has a lot of cacti. I grow cacti at home. They grow very slowly. I
	have one that is nearly six feet tall. I wouldn't mind living in Arizona.
	I think it would be fun to live in a desert. Deserts have interesting
	animals.

There are several problems with the way Monica answered the question. The most serious one is that she doesn't answer the question that is asked. She writes about why Dean and Lorna moved to Arizona, not about what they missed about the East Coast. She also writes about growing cacti and that she would like to live in Arizona. She doesn't stay on target. She doesn't answer the question that is asked.

ANSWERING ALL PARTS OF THE QUESTION

It is important that you make sure you answer all parts of the question.

See how Therese answered question 1C.

1C. **How did Dean and Lorna feel about living in Arizona? How did their lives change after Dean went online? Use details from the passage to support your answer.**

Therese's answer:

	Dean and Lorna didn't like Arizona because they missed the East
	Coast. The desert was very dry, and they didn't have a lawn or
	trees that had leaves that changed color and dropped off. They
	were used to living near the ocean, where it rains a lot. They felt
	dry all the time in Arizona, like raisins or lizards, because it didn't
	rain very much.

The first part of this answer is fine. But Therese didn't answer the second part of the question. She needs to include information about how Dean's and Lorna's lives changed after Dean went online.

A possible answer to the second part of the question might be:

	After Dean went online, he learned about a palace in Spain where
	they had fountains and streams and used recycled water. Dean
	designed his own fountain with a sprinkler and a pool. He and Lorna
	would run under the sprinkler, and it felt like rain to them. They were
	both much happier after this.

USING THE INFORMATION FROM THE SELECTION

The open-ended questions on the test usually remind you to use information from the selection. This is very important. When you take information from the story or article, use actual details.

Read Freddy's and Javon's answers to the next question and decide which student uses information from the selection.

1D. **Why did Dean want to build a fountain? Support your answer with details from the passage.**

Freddy's answer:

	Dean wanted to build a fountain. I like fountains. I like to watch the
	water spray out of them. I like sprinklers too. I use the sprinkler
	when it is hot, and I like to spray my younger brother with the hose.

Javon's answer:

	Dean wanted to build a fountain. He loved all kinds of water. When he
	lived near the ocean, he would go swimming in the rain. He liked to
	watch the rain fall. He and Lorna felt like raisins or lizards because
	it was so dry in the desert.

Which person used more information from the story?

A   **Freddy**

B   **Javon**

Your teacher will discuss your answer.

USING SUPPORTING DETAILS

Stories usually have a lot of details. When you write your open-ended answer, make sure to use details to support your topic.

Read Natalie's and Sondra's answers to the next question.

1E. Why did Lorna and Dean miss the East Coast? Support your answer with details from the passage.

Natalie's answer:

	Lorna and Dean missed the East Coast. They liked having a front	
	lawn and trees with leaves that changed color and fell off.	

Sondra's answer:

	Lorna and Dean missed the East Coast. They moved to Arizona	
	because Dean had allergies. He felt better in Arizona. They lived in	
	Arizona for two years.	

1. Both Natalie and Sondra used details from the story. Which person used the best supporting details?

_____ **Natalie**

_____ **Sondra**

 Your teacher will discuss your answer.

STRATEGIES AND TIPS
FOR WRITING ANSWERS TO OPEN-ENDED QUESTIONS

1   Be sure that:

❧   you answer the question that is asked

❧   you answer all parts of the question

❧   you include details and examples from the story

❧   you use supporting details

❧   you stay on target

2   Be sure that you do NOT:

❧   answer with just one or two words

SELECTIONS FOR PRACTICE

SELECTION 1

Some people are specialists. They know everything about one specific topic, like car brakes or honeybees. Other people are interested in a great many things.

The twentieth and twenty-first centuries are largely an age of specialists. The broad, general education of the past—the type of education that Thomas Jefferson had—in which students and adults past their school years sought to learn as much as they could about their world is, by and large, a thing of the past. Today, it is rare for anyone to be fluent in a wide range of subjects. The man or woman who masters a single science or art is considered an accomplished person.

Thomas Jefferson was one of our greatest presidents, but politics was only one of the subjects he mastered. He was anything but a specialist. He was interested in almost everything there was to learn. He had his own museum for his collection of fossils. His personal library, with over 10,000 volumes, was one of the largest of his time. He could speak Italian, Spanish, French, Latin, and Greek with ease. He was also the architect of his own home, Monticello, one of the most beautiful structures of his time. In addition, he was a pioneer in agriculture, inventing a new kind of plow.

Jefferson was as brilliant and versatile in his public life as he was in his personal life. He was the principal author of the Declaration of Independence. He introduced into the law of Virginia the concepts that church and state should be separate and that no law should dictate what a person's religion should be. He was a diplomat in France, the governor of Virginia, the founder of the University of Virginia, and, of course, the president of the United States.

1A. Why would Jefferson not be considered a specialist? Use details from the article to support your answer.

_____

_____

_____

_____

_____

_____

1B. The article says that Jefferson was as brilliant and versatile in his public life as he was in his personal life. Why does the author say this? Use details from the article to support your answer.

_____

_____

_____

_____

_____

_____

SELECTION 2

A DOUBLE LIFE

a science fiction story by Shelley Fields

Graduation was in a few days. Everyone in William's class wanted mementos to remember their friends when they went on to their new schools. Three people were waiting for William to sign their autograph books. He was too rushed to write a note in each one, so he just signed his name. William was always complaining that there wasn't enough time.

Keesha looked at the autograph book that William had just returned to her. "David Prescott? Who is that?" she said in surprise. William looked at his signature. It was right there, plain as day. Instead of writing William Brown, he had signed the book "David Prescott."

"You did the same thing to me," said Lawrence. "Look here, it says David Prescott."

William was puzzled. Why would he sign somebody else's name? For the rest of the day he paid careful attention when he signed his name.

When William got home from school, he forgot about the incident. He had to do his homework and help around the house. He didn't think of it again until the next morning, when he woke up from a very strange dream.

William dreamed that he lived in a different city with a different family and was going to a different school. Although he had a sister and a brother, in his dream family there were four boys and no girls. The father in the dream was a lot taller than his real father. There didn't seem to be a mother around. And in his dream, his name was David Prescott.

After that, William had the same kind of dream every night. At first the strange dreams bothered him, but after a while he began to look forward to them. He liked the life, the family, the school, house, and friends in his dreams. William couldn't decide which he liked more, his dream life as David or his daytime life as William.

One evening William was watching television when he saw a familiar face. An important scientist was being interviewed on a news program. He said he was working on a theory about time and space. He believed that certain people could live in two worlds instead of just one. The scientist, a Dr. Meecham, looked exactly like William's dream father. Dr. Meecham invited everyone to hear him speak at the university the next day.

William sat in the audience at the university and listened with amazement. Meecham looked and talked exactly like the man he called Dad in his dreams every night. Meecham told the audience that more than one world could exist in the same space at the same time. He called them "parallel universes." If one could discover the path between the two worlds, a person could have more than one life.

Now William understood what had been happening at night. He was living two lives, in two different universes. When Dr. Meecham finished his lecture, William pushed his way to the front of the auditorium.

Dr. Meecham was speaking with some people. When William caught his eye, Dr. Meecham looked surprised. But it was clear that he recognized William. He interrupted his conversation for a moment and told William they would have to speak later. Then he resumed his conversation with the other people.

William couldn't wait to get to sleep that night. In his dream the man known as Dr. Meecham was Arthur Prescott. Arthur Prescott worked in a bank. And when William was David, he couldn't remember what had happened during the day. He couldn't remember being William.

William thought it would be easy to find Dr. Meecham again, but it wasn't. He called the university and learned that Dr. Meecham had been a guest speaker the day he heard him. He had almost given up when he saw Dr. Meecham walking down the stairs of the public library.

"Dr. Meecham, or Dad, or whoever you are, please tell me what's going on," William begged.

Meecham looked deep into William's eyes and then laughed. "Guess I'm going to have to level with you, son," he said. "I'm a lucky person. I can travel between the two worlds and remember. Seems like you are lucky, too."

Dr. Meecham explained to William that many people live in both universes, but only a few know that they do. The secret is to find the path. To get back and forth between the worlds, you can never completely sleep. Your body has to sleep or you will get sick, but a little part of you must always stay awake.

In the other world, Meecham spent his time as Arthur Prescott. Arthur Prescott worked in a bank and raised some fine boys. His wife had died a few years back. In this world he was Dr. Charles Meecham, a scientist. He didn't have a wife or children.

William asked Dr. Meecham if he remembered this world when he was in the other. "Remembering is the path between the worlds," Dr. Meecham explained. "If you remember in both worlds and use your time in both well, very interesting things will happen."

"How can I learn to stay a little awake even when I sleep? How can I remember in both worlds?" asked William.

Dr. Meecham laughed. "That's for you to figure out."

That was a few years ago. William never had a problem remembering his dream world as David Prescott. He is just learning to remember being William when he is in David's world. It still isn't easy for him to use the path, but his life has grown rich. He is using his time in an interesting way. In one world he is learning Spanish, in the other French. In one world he plays the guitar, in the other, the piano.

In one world he is class president, in the other he spends most of his time at his computer.

Whether he is called William or David, he finds there still isn't enough time to do all the things he wants to do.

2A. Dr. Meecham told William that it was important to stay awake a little bit even when you sleep. Why did he tell William that? Use details from the story in writing your answer.

_____

_____

_____

_____

_____

_____

2B. What good things happened to William as a result of living in two different worlds? Use details from the story to support your answer.

_____

_____

_____

_____

_____

_____

PART 2

READING

NOTICE: Photocopying any part of this book is forbidden by law.

21

2

CENTRAL IDEA

MAIN IDEA

The **main idea** is the most important idea of a selection. It is sometimes called the **central idea** or the **central topic**. The main idea is developed or strengthened by other ideas called **supporting ideas**.

Read Example 1. Decide which is the main idea and which are the supporting ideas.

EXAMPLE 1

I won't buy that coat. The style is old-fashioned, and besides, it costs too much. That's how I feel about it.

1. Write **MI** opposite the main idea.

   Write **SI** opposite the supporting idea.

   A   I won't buy that coat. _____

   B   The style is old-fashioned. _____

   C   It costs too much. _____

I won't buy that coat is the main idea. The rest of the paragraph helps us understand why the writer won't buy the coat. Therefore **A** is the main idea, and B and C are supporting ideas.

IRRELEVANT DETAILS

Sometimes a selection contains ideas or facts that don't have much to do with the main idea. These ideas are called **not relevant**, or **irrelevant**.

Read the next example, determine the main idea, and then decide which information is not relevant to the main idea.

EXAMPLE 2

People came to America for many reasons in the early 1800s. Some came to find religious freedom, some came to get rich, some came to escape from poverty and starvation. Many came against their will, brought here as slaves. Museums contain excellent paintings of these early settlers.

The main idea is: *People came to America for many reasons.*

2. Which information is least relevant or least useful in helping us understand the main idea?

   A   Some came for religious freedom.

   B   Slaves came against their will.

   C   Museums have paintings of early settlers.

   D   People came to escape poverty.

 Your teacher will discuss your answer.

DEVELOPING THE MAIN IDEA WITH SUPPORTING DETAILS

Irrelevant information may be interesting or amusing, but it does not help us understand the central thesis. On the other hand, some supporting ideas may be very important in building our understanding of the main idea. These ideas are said to **develop the main idea** or to be **subordinate to the main idea**.

EXAMPLE 3

Pablo Picasso was one of the most gifted artists in history—a painter and sculptor who created masterworks in almost every medium and who has been a major influence on the history of art. He was born in Spain, but lived most of his life in France. He hated war and sought to show how evil it was through his work. His masterwork *Guernica* depicted the horror of war in almost unbearable intensity.

3. The main idea is: *Picasso was a gifted artist.* **Which idea best develops the main idea?**

   A Picasso hated war.

   B Picasso was born in Spain.

   C He created masterworks in almost every medium.

   D His greatest masterpiece was *Guernica.*

The correct choice is **C**, *He created masterworks in almost every medium.* Choice A tells us Picasso hated war. This is important information, but it does not tell us as much about why he was a gifted artist as choice C does. Choice B is not relevant. Choice D is a fairly good answer because it tells us something about Picasso's work, but it does not develop the main idea as well as choice C.

In the next section you will practice using these skills. Questions will be worded many different ways, but there are really only three types of questions.

1   Identify the **main idea** or **most important point**.

   or

2   Identify information **least relevant** to the central thesis.

   or

3   Select ideas which **best develop** the central theme.

STRATEGIES AND TIPS
FOR IDENTIFYING CENTRAL IDEA AND SUPPORTING DETAILS

1   After you read a selection, ask, "What was the story about?" Try to sum up your answer in a single sentence. This is the **main idea**.

2   Don't confuse a story detail with the main idea. Details help tell you about the main idea. They develop the main idea.

3   Some information is irrelevant to the main idea. It does not develop the central topic.

SELECTIONS FOR PRACTICE

SELECTION 1

W&W service provides one of the cheapest and most effective ways to meet new people and to advertise new services. The W&W procedure for sending a message is the height of simplicity. You write a note, insert it in a bottle, and throw the bottle into the ocean. The wind and water (hence the name W&W) carry the message to all sorts of unexpected places and thereby help the note writer to publicize his or her message.

Arthur Sandpur tried this technique one lonely Saturday morning. He collected 990 old bottles and inserted a note in each of them, saying he wanted to meet some new friends. As a consequence he received 34 replies from all over the world, including many invitations to parties, and found himself with a rich social life. Businesses have also been successful with the W&W service. The Yacht Repair Corporation, which is located in California, tossed 100 bottles into the sea and wound up with several important new customers. The W&W service really works.

1. The main idea of this selection is contained in the first sentence. Which information best supports the main idea?

    A   Arthur Sandpur received many replies to his message.

    B   No one can tell where the bottle will land.

    C   The Yacht Repair Corporation is located in California.

    D   W&W stands for wind and water.

SELECTION 2

Many early American explorers suffered personal disaster. Columbus was sent home in chains. LaSalle, who explored the Mississippi River, was murdered by his own men. Verrazano may have been hanged as a pirate. Pizarro became a multimillionaire by conquering Peru but was eventually killed by a group of soldiers. Balboa, who discovered the Pacific Ocean, was murdered as well.

2. Which information least supports the main idea of the selection?

   A   Balboa was murdered.

   B   Columbus was sent home in chains.

   C   Pizarro became a multimillionaire.

   D   Verrazano may have been hanged.

SELECTION 3

In this selection, which comes from the great African American writer Maya Angelou's Wouldn't Take Nothing for My Journey Now, *her grandmother is speaking to her.*

"Sister, there are people who went to sleep all over the world last night, rich and poor and white and black, but they will never wake again. Sister, those who expected to rise did not, their beds became their cooling boards, and their blankets became their winding sheets. And those dead folks would give anything at all for just five minutes of this weather or ten minutes of that plowing that person was grumbling about. So you watch yourself about complaining, Sister. What you're supposed to do when you don't like a thing is change it. If you can't change it, change the way you think about it. Don't complain."

3. What is the main idea of this selection?

   A   A person shouldn't complain.

   B   Everything can be changed.

   C   People are better off after they die.

   D   Some people never wake up.

SELECTION 4

Cotton is a warm-climate crop. To mature, the plant needs a growing season of about 150 days free of frost. Most parts of the country do not offer such a long period of warmth, and so cotton is grown in only a few states. In our country, various attempts have been made to grow cotton outside the South, but these attempts have generally proved unsuccessful because of weather conditions. However, cotton is grown in 60 warm-weather countries outside the United States. More and more cotton farmers are mechanized and have replaced the traditional mule-drawn planters with automated equipment.

4. Which fact LEAST supports the main thesis?

A   A brief spell of cold weather kills the cotton plant.

B   Cotton is grown in warm countries around the world.

C   Cotton needs a growing season of 150 days without frost.

D   Mechanized farmers outnumber traditional mule-drawn planters.

SELECTION 5

The mole spends most of its life in darkness. It lives in an underground burrow and tunnels through the earth to find its food of earthworms. A long ridge of earth that zigzags across lawn and field is probably the roof of a mole's tunnel. The creature that makes this tunnel is only about six inches long, with a naked pink tail about an inch long and dense, velvety, mouse-colored fur. Moles disfigure lawns and gardens with the ridges they make. For that reason, many people do not like to have moles living on their property. But moles do pay for some of the damage by eating cutworms and other root-destroying pests as well as earthworms.

5. The main idea of this selection is that

    A   moles are only six inches long.

    B   moles live underground and disfigure lawns.

    C   moles have pink tails.

    D   moles have mouse-colored fur.

SELECTION 6

A person who has been arrested has many important legal rights, including the right to remain silent without penalty. An arrested person may demand the opportunity to confer with an attorney without any danger that the exercise of the right to counsel will be construed as an admission of guilt. Furthermore, the accused person may require legal authorities to provide a detailed statement of his legal rights. Needless to say, in all such proceedings the accused should remain courteous. An abusive tone is not conducive to good treatment.

6. Which statement is LEAST effective in developing the central idea?

    A   The accused has the right to remain silent.

    B   The accused should remain courteous.

    C   The accused may confer with an attorney.

    D   The accused may hear his legal rights.

3

SEQUENCE

SEQUENCE AND KEY WORDS

In everyday life, events occur one after another. It's the same in anything you read. The order in which events occur is known as the sequence of events. In writing, the **sequence of events** is sometimes shown by **key words** or phrases that make the order clear.

In the following example, determine the order in which Devon did things.

EXAMPLE 1

First Devon skied down to the scene of the accident. *Then* he called for a medi-vac helicopter to come to the end of the slope. *Finally*, he supervised the airlifting of the injured skier to the hospital.

1. Write 1, 2, and 3 next to the events that happened in this example so that they are in the correct order.

   A _____ called for a helicopter

   B _____ supervised the airlifting of the skier

   C _____ raced to the scene of the accident

The events in the example happened in the order **C A B**. Here the key words used to show the order of events are:

First

Then

Finally

Some other key words that may indicate sequence are:

- *Later* in the day . . .
- *After* completing the job . . .
- *Last*, he waved and left.
- *Before* they were married . . .
- *Prior* to the meeting . . .
- *Sometime thereafter*, when the leaves were falling . . .

Sometimes a selection does not include key words, but you can determine the sequence of events from other clues. Common clues are times (for example, *6:30 p.m.*); calendar dates (for example, *June 14, 1995*); terms such as *today, tomorrow, yesterday*; seasons; or parts of the day (for example, *It was just turning dark . . .*)

Read the next example and look closely at the sequence of events.

EXAMPLE 2

Liana wanted to make a special treat for her mother's birthday. In the morning, she looked through several cookbooks until she found a recipe that sounded good—a dark chocolate cake with coconut. Later in the day, she went to the store to buy the ingredients. When she got home she preheated the oven. She mixed the batter and poured it into a pan. She put the cake in the oven. While she was waiting for the cake to bake, she made the frosting. Just before dinner, she tested the cake by sticking it with a toothpick. When the toothpick came out dry, she took the pan from the oven and let the cake cool. She frosted the entire cake and then sprinkled it with coconut. Just before her mother got home, she hid the cake. Then, when everyone was finished eating, Liana brought out her beautiful cake. "Happy Birthday!" she said.

2. What was the first thing that Liana did?

    A   She went to the store.

    B   She put the cake in the oven.

    C   She found a good recipe.

    D   She took the pan from the oven.

Your teacher will discuss your answer.

IMPLIED SEQUENCE

Sometimes the clues used for determining sequence are not in key words or in words about time. Instead, they are found in the logic of the way things happen in the world. You have to use your own knowledge of the world around you to figure out what must have happened.

EXAMPLE 3

Maria has two friends, Carla and Peter. She met Carla when she was learning to drive a car, but she has known Peter since nursery school.

3A. Whom has she known longer?

    A   Carla

    B   Peter

3B. How do you know that?

_____

_____

_____

_____

_____

_____

Logic tells you Maria has known Peter longer, since you most likely are not in nursery school when you learn to drive a car.

STRATEGIES AND TIPS
FOR DETERMINING SEQUENCE

1   Look for key words that show the **sequence of events** in a selection.

2   Other words and phrases may provide clues to the time at which events took place.

3   If there are no key words or other clues in the wording of a selection, you should be able to figure out the order of events from logical connections between the things that happened.

SELECTIONS FOR PRACTICE

SELECTION 1

There were hurricane warnings on the news. A police officer came to the Tilmans' home to ask them to leave until the storm had passed. The family was going to have to evacuate. Before they abandoned their house for the duration of the storm, they did everything they could to protect it. First they took large pieces of plywood and boarded up the windows. Then they brought all their outside furniture into the house. After that, they packed the car with all their valuables, their family pictures, and other treasures. Right before they left, they put their remaining possessions in bathrooms and closets, rooms that would receive the least damage. Then they were ready.

1. Which of the following did the Tilman family do LAST?

   A   They boarded up the windows with plywood.

   B   They packed the car with their valuables.

   C   They brought their outside furniture inside.

   D   They put their remaining possessions in bathrooms and closets.

SELECTION 2

Jessica played her first tennis game with Tim. She made All-State in high school the month after she was introduced to Philip. Now she is the star player at the university.

2. What clues tell you that Jessica knew Tim longer than Philip?

   _____

   _____

   _____

   _____

   _____

   _____

   _____

SELECTION 3

Andrew wanted to get his driver's license so he wouldn't have to depend on friends or family to take him everywhere. It took three months, a lot of practice, and two tries at the driving test, but he finally did get his license. His friend Hal taught him to drive. They went out almost every day. When Andrew took his first test, he wasn't able to parallel park, and he slid through a stop sign. The second test went better, and the inspector approved him. Andrew was very grateful to his friend for helping him, so, right after he got his license, he drove to the mall and bought Hal a great new CD.

3. Which happened LAST?

   A   Hal taught Andrew to drive.

   B   Andrew bought a CD for Hal.

   C   Andrew passed his test.

   D   Andrew slid through a stop sign.

SELECTION 4

Jesse wanted to pass on the expertise he had gained, to help others to develop the skills and self-confidence he had acquired. He remembered the bitter period in the hospital when he felt he had lost forever the joy and exultation that competition in sports had provided him. He remembered how difficult it had been for him to learn to use a wheelchair and crutches. Then he remembered the unexpected delight he had discovered from developing new skills in his wheelchair, the thrill of once again moving down the field, of once again using all his skills to the limit of his body's capability. He wanted to work with those men and women who had lost the hope that they could ever compete again, and to teach them how much they could still do.

4A. Jesse participated in sports

    A   both before and after being in the hospital.

    B   only after learning to use a wheelchair.

    C   only before he was hospitalized.

    D   when he was first hospitalized.

4B. What clues in the story help you figure this out?

_____

_____

_____

_____

_____

_____

4

CAUSE AND EFFECT

When reading a story, we often want to know the **cause** or reason why something happened. We may also want to know what happened as a result of an event. This is called the **effect**.

Often cause and effect relationships can be identified by key words or phrases.

* ❖ *Because* we were late to class, we . . .
* ❖ *Since* the phone was ringing, Sue . . .
* ❖ *The main reason* the law was passed . . .
* ❖ Three families were homeless *as a result of* the fire.

Use a key word to determine the cause in the following example.

EXAMPLE 1

My friends and I followed the stranger down Ellis Street. We were suspicious since we had never seen him before. He could tell we were following him, and he looked back once or twice. At the intersection with Main Avenue, he started talking to Sergeant Firpo of our police department. He was Sergeant Firpo's brother, and we were really embarrassed!

1. The narrator and the narrator's friends were suspicious of the stranger because
   A   he was talking to Sergeant Firpo.
   B   he kept looking back.
   C   they had never seen him before.
   D   he embarrassed them.

The second sentence gives the reason for their suspicion, beginning with the key word *since*. The correct answer is **C**.

IMPLIED CAUSE AND EFFECT

Many cause-and-effect relationships do not use key words. You will not find words like *because* or *therefore* or *so* in the next selection. The relationship is **implied**, with no key words to guide you.

EXAMPLE 2

The usual diet for tigers and leopards is large animals. In order to catch these animals, tigers and leopards have to be fast, and their claws and teeth have to be in good shape. However, when a tiger or leopard has been slowed down by age or by painful wounds, or when some of its teeth are missing and its claws are worn down, it may begin to seek easier prey, like smaller animals that have been wounded or that are sick. Older tigers and leopards may even attack human beings for food. Humans make easy victims for a worn-out tiger or leopard. Even so, a tiger or leopard's first human kill usually occurs by accident. The animal may be lying in the tall jungle grass when an unsuspecting person comes along. The surprise meeting which follows is one that neither the person nor the animal expected or wanted. The animal feels cornered; it attacks and kills the human. When the animal realizes how easy it is to kill a human, it is likely it will attack humans again.

2. Why do tigers and leopards begin attacking sick animals and human beings?

_____

_____

_____

_____

_____

_____

   Your teacher will discuss your answer.

So far you have looked at causes—the reasons why things happen. The next example asks you to look for an effect.

EXAMPLE 3

Australia, the continent that lies between the equator and the South Pole, is sometimes called the "land down under," because of its location below the equator. In Australia, the weather in the north is much warmer than the weather in the south, because northern Australia lies nearer to the equator. In fact, the extreme north is a jungle area where much rain falls. The eastern and central plains of Australia have good farmland and grazing areas, but father west, the climate gets hotter and drier until finally there is just desert land. Toward the west coast, the climate becomes moderate again.

Since Australia lies below the equator, it is in the Southern Hemisphere, and its seasons occur at the opposite time from those in the Northern Hemisphere. June, July, and August are Australia's winter months; its summer months are December, January, and February. In Australia, however, winters are mild and the sun is always shining. In the city of Sydney, located on the east coast, the temperature on a winter day rarely drops below 60 degrees.

3. Which of these is NOT an effect of Australia's being located south of the equator?

    A It is called the "land down under."

    B The seasons are the opposite of seasons in the northern hemisphere.

    C The south is colder than the north.

    D There is good farmland in the central plains.

Statements A, B, and C are effects of Australia's location south of the equator. Only **D** is a fact that has nothing to do with the continent's location in relation to the equator.

STRATEGIES AND TIPS
FOR DETERMINING CAUSE AND EFFECT

1   Look for key words that signal **cause** and **effect**. The words that follow the key word or phrase will explain what caused something or what its effect was.

2   When there are no key words, ask yourself why an event happened (its cause) or what happened as a result of an event (its effect).

3   Try to decide what the logical cause or effect of an event would be. Look for the cause or effect in the passage.

SELECTIONS FOR PRACTICE

SELECTION 1

At one time, the autumn air used to be thick with the smell of burning leaves. Piles of them, orange, yellow and brown, lined the curbs of neighborhood streets. While they burned, the smoke filled the air with a distinctive scent. Inside, the houses were warmed by burning logs. The smoke from the fireplaces wafted up the chimneys, joining the smoke from the leaves and making a wonderful autumn haze.

Then it was discovered that the smoke was polluting the air. Many parts of the country banned the burning of fall leaves. Fireplace fires were discouraged. Unfortunately, one kind of pollution is replacing another. Now the sound of leaf blowers disturbs the fall calm.

1. According to this article, why don't people burn leaves anymore?

    A   The fires are dangerous.

    B   The smoke pollutes the air.

    C   Leaf blowers are much better.

    D   They burned them in the fireplace.

SELECTION 2

Denzel was getting bad grades in math. He liked math, but he never quite got it. He was a good student otherwise. His parents were understanding, but they told him he needed to do better or he wouldn't be able to play basketball after school.

Frederick, a boy in Denzel's class, was great at math. He wasn't so good at basketball. Denzel offered to trade lessons. He would help Frederick play basketball better if Frederick would help him learn math. They made an agreement, and it worked. Denzel's math grades shot up. In a little while, Denzel and Frederick were playing basketball together after school.

2. What was the effect of the agreement made by Denzel and Frederick?

    A   Denzel was punished for his poor math grades.

    B   Frederick made money as a tutor.

    C   Each learned something from the other.

    D   They started playing basketball on the school team.

SELECTION 3

The castor tree happened accidentally, too. An old castor tree was growing in the yard of our neighbors across the alley. One summer some of its seeds got into our yard, and the following summer we had a small castor tree of our own. It was a spurious sort of a tree, growing much too rapidly and being much too delicate for a tree. A small boy couldn't climb it and the least little storm that came along would tear some of its branches away. But it had a nice leaf and a clean growing odor and it made a lot of shade.

—from "The Broken Wheel" by William Saroyan

3. Why did the castor tree grow in the narrator's yard?

   A   It was actually growing in his neighbor's alley.

   B   A storm tore off some branches.

   C   His father planted it.

   D   A seed from a neighbor's tree took root and grew.

SELECTION 4

In the sandy Sahara Desert, a place that is fertile and green because of an underground stream is called an oasis. It is only at an oasis that a person who travels across the Sahara can find water. In the Sahara, however, windstorms are almost as great a danger as the shortage of water. Windstorms change the surface of the desert continually. The wind blows sand into waves and peaks, leaving valleys where there were once sand dunes and changing flat areas into hill areas. Because the surface of the desert is changing all the time, there are no landmarks; travelers need to guide themselves by the stars at night and rest during the hot daylight hours.

4. Why are windstorms a greater danger than water shortage in the Sahara?

_____

_____

_____

_____

_____

_____

5

AUTHOR'S VIEWPOINT

An **author's viewpoint** about a subject affects everything that he or she writes. An alert reader should be aware of the author's viewpoint, and should be conscious of how the author makes that viewpoint known. Sometimes it will be clearly stated. At other times, you can get a good idea of the author's feelings from the language used, the examples given, and the way the selection is put together.

In the following example the author discusses a play she saw. Decide what the author's opinion of the movie is.

EXAMPLE 1

Although *Good Life* is a well-written and humorous play, its portrayal of life is far too simplistic. The central characters are desperate to become rich and powerful. They do so, but the way in which they attain their goals isn't very likely in today's world. We are asked to accept a number of situations that could never exist.

Although the acting is sometimes brilliant, the sets imaginative, and the directing clear, the view of life is at best two-dimensional and would benefit from a rewrite.

1. Overall, what does the author think about the play?

    A   It is a great play in all respects.

    B   It portrays believable situations.

    C   It needs a lot of work.

    D   Its good qualities far outweigh a few bad points.

Choice C is correct. Although the selection includes positive statements, overall the author provides a negative appraisal. Even though many aspects of the play are praised, we can conclude the overall view is not positive. based on the statement that the play would benefit from a rewrite.

Read the next example and decide how the author feels about gossip.

EXAMPLE 2

Gwyn walked outside one day and saw a large truck in front of the Holdens' house. She decided that they must be moving. Gwyn told her friend Marina that the Holdens were moving. Marina thought that they must be moving to Texas because that's where they were from. She told Paul that the Holdens were moving back to Texas. Paul figured that, since they were moving, Mr. Holden must be going back to his old job. He told his father that Mr. Holden was taking back his old job in Texas. Paul's father worked with Mr. Holden. He told their boss that Mr. Holden was quitting his job for a job in Texas.

Mr. Holden's boss was very angry because Mr. Holden hadn't told him. He called him into his office, ready to fire Mr. Holden before he quit. Mr. Holden told him he wasn't leaving. He told his boss that the truck was there because his mother was moving in with him.

Mr. Holden was upset that someone was spreading rumors that had caused trouble for him with his boss, but he didn't even know where the rumors had begun.

2.   What point is the author trying to make?

_____

_____

_____

_____

_____

   Your teacher will discuss your answer.

STRATEGIES AND TIPS
FOR DETERMINING AUTHOR'S VIEWPOINT

1   Look for negative or positive words that indicate the author's attitude.

2   Decide what feelings you have after reading the passage. Your reaction may be what the author intended you to feel about the topic.

3   Look at the examples or details that the author provides. Do these examples suggest a particular viewpoint of the topic?

SELECTIONS FOR PRACTICE

SELECTION 1

Although baseball is an interesting and extremely popular sport, it provides much less effective exercise than other sports. In contrast to baseball, soccer is a sport that exercises the entire body. Although running is important in both of these sports, the athlete playing soccer is able to run for longer periods without interruption, thereby providing a more effective workout. Baseball is, however, fun to watch, and a good sport for television viewing.

1.   The author feels that baseball

    A   is boring but good exercise.

    B   is boring and does not provide effective exercise.

    C   is interesting and provides effective exercise.

    D   is interesting but does not provide effective exercise.

SELECTION 2

For a number of years, people have been pointing out that human beings are more destructive than most wild animals. They use war and crime as examples of human behavior in contrast to how animals behave among themselves. They also show examples of animals that mate for life and compare it to the high divorce rate among humans.

However, animal observers have found that mating for life is extremely rare among animals. They have also noted that violent behavior within a species' own breed is not uncommon. Even the beloved dolphin has been shown to misbehave.

2. What is the author trying to say in this article?

    A   Animals are better to each other than people.

    B   Both wild animals and humans can act badly.

    C   Humans are better to each other than animals.

    D   All creatures can behave well.

SELECTION 3

Some people think that SUVs, or sport utility vehicles, are safe to drive. It is true that if another car hits one of them, the SUV will sustain less damage. But there is another question. What about the cars they hit? The bumper on most SUVs is located where it can do a lot of damage to a smaller car. Also, the sheer size of one of those large four-wheel-drive vehicles will make it the winner in any road competition with a smaller vehicle, should an accident occur. Is it fair that one vehicle should be larger and safer at the expense of smaller, less protected cars?

3. **What point is the author trying to make?**

_____

_____

_____

_____

_____

_____

SELECTION 4

It was rush hour. The platform was jammed with people trying to get a spot to board the incoming train. Jim pushed his way inside. Someone managed to step on his foot, nearly crippling him. The air inside was stiflingly hot. He was squished up next to a woman who kept glaring at him. The walls of the train were painted an awful shade of green. Suddenly the smells made him sick to his stomach. He didn't know if he could last until his stop.

4. **The author's portrayal makes the subway ride seem**

    A   extremely unpleasant.

    B   a lot of fun.

    C   mostly exhilarating.

    D   no worse than most experiences.

NOTICE: Photocopying any part of this book is forbidden by law.

47

ANALYZING CHARACTERS

In order to understand a story, you must understand the people in it. People give a story its meaning. The people in the story are called **characters**.

A writer may portray a character in flattering terms or in a negative fashion. Details may include the character's appearance and way of moving and speaking. The writer may also tell about a character's actions, statements, and thoughts, and the kind of relationships the character has with other people, to give you a sense of who a character is.

Read the following example. How does the author portray Toni?

EXAMPLE 1

Toni really enjoyed living with her mother in their little apartment. There was only one bedroom, so she slept on the pullout coach in the living room. They didn't have much, but she and her mother always had a good time. Then things changed. Her mother became sick and was hospitalized. Toni had to move in with her aunt miles away.

She missed her mother and their little apartment. Her aunt was nice enough, but they didn't have much to say to each other. She missed the friends she had in her old building and at her school. She didn't know anyone in the new town.

1. How would you describe Toni?

   A bored

   B happy

   C mean

   D lonely

The best choice is **D**. Toni was in a new town and didn't know anyone. She missed her friends. She was lonely.

Sometimes an author uses adjectives like *friendly* or *nervous* to describe people. At other times, the author describes how characters act without using descriptive words like *scared* or *stubborn*. You can still figure out what these people are like from how they act. Read the next example and decide what kind of person Timothy is.

EXAMPLE 2

Timothy got upset pretty easily. If the teacher didn't call on him when he raised his hand, he might stomp out of the room. If he didn't get the present he wanted on his birthday, he sometimes threw what he got on the floor. If someone said something he disagreed with, he sometimes sulked.

2. Timothy could be described as

   A easy going.

   B friendly.

   C bad tempered.

   D patient.

 Your teacher will discuss your answer.

HOW CHARACTERS CHANGE

Sometimes you are asked how a character changes during the course of a story. Read Example 3 and decide how Fred changes.

EXAMPLE 3

Fred was a slave to his nervous habits, always tapping his pencil on his desk or tearing up bits of paper. Sometimes he bit his nails or cracked his knuckles. He would jingle the coins in his pocket anxiously. The habits didn't bother him much and didn't bother other people either—until he tried out for the band.

Fred played the trumpet quite well. But when he got up to audition for the band, he jingled the coins in his pocket, he tapped his foot loudly on the floor, and he bit his nails.

The leader of the band told Fred that he would have to stop being so jittery. Fred tried to control his habits. It wasn't easy, and at first he failed miserably. He worried he would be thrown out of the band. Finally, he came up with an idea. He stopped carrying coins in his pocket so he couldn't jingle them. He kept his hands on his trumpet at all times, so he wouldn't bite his nails. He wore shoes with extra-thick, soft rubber soles that wouldn't make so much noise when he tapped. After a while he overcame his nervousness and learned to relax. He no longer felt the need to jingle coins, bite his nails, or make other kinds of disturbances. Still he continued to tap his foot. He realized that almost all the band members tapped their feet to keep time.

3. How did Fred change?
   A   He got to be in a good band.
   B   He controlled his habits.
   C   He never tapped his feet.
   D   He became a worse musician.

Choice **B** is the correct answer. The important change for Fred, after which other things changed, was controlling his habits.

COMPARING AND CONTRASTING CHARACTERS

Sometimes you are asked to *compare* one character with another. Decide in what ways the characters in the following selection are alike or different.

EXAMPLE 4

Sondra and Felicity were sisters and best friends. They enjoyed reading the same books and going to the same movies. They spent all their free time listening to the same music. But if you called their house, you always knew which one you had on the phone. Sondra would never say more than was necessary, especially about herself. If you asked how she was, she always told you she was fine. If you asked her what was happening, she always answered, "Not much."

On the other hand, if you were speaking with Felicity, you might hear about every mosquito bite she had. She would tell you how many hours she had slept the night before and if she had a good breakfast. You always knew her mood, if she was up or down. Sondra was more of a mystery.

4. How did Felicity and Sondra differ?

_____

_____

_____

_____

_____

_____

Your teacher will discuss your answer.

STRATEGIES AND TIPS
FOR UNDERSTANDING CHARACTER

1 Look for parts of a story that tell you how a character acts and relates to other people.

2 Find the words and phrases that describe the character.

3 See how a character changes during the course of a story.

4 Sometimes there are two important characters in the story. Decide how they are alike and how they are different.

SELECTIONS FOR PRACTICE

SELECTION 1

Everyone in the neighborhood knew Mr. Galsworthy. He took a walk at exactly 6:00 every evening, smiling and saying "Hello" and nothing else to everyone he passed. No one ever saw him act anything but friendly, but no one ever learned anything more about him. He left for work at 8:00 every morning, and at 11:00 p.m. every evening, the lights went out in his house.

1. How is Mr. Galsworthy described in this passage?

    A   mean, hostile, withdrawn

    B   quiet, friendly, regular in his habits

    C   wild and out of control

    D   unwilling to have anything to do with his neighbors

SELECTION 2

This selection comes from Anne Frank: The Diary of a Young Girl, *a recounting of the life of a young girl who was in hiding from the Nazis, with her family and others, during World War II.*

I can't seem to sit still lately; I run upstairs and down and then back again. I love talking to Peter, but I'm always afraid of being a nuisance. He has told me a bit about the past, about his parents and about himself. It's not half enough and I ask myself why it is that I always long for more. He used to think I was unbearable; and I returned the compliment; now I have changed my opinion, has he changed his too?

I think so; still it doesn't necessarily mean that we shall become great friends, although as far as I am concerned it would make the time here much more bearable.

2. In this selection Anne Frank seems to be

   A starting to like Peter a lot.

   B getting quieter as she gets older.

   C ready to bother people all the time.

   D enjoying becoming older.

SELECTION 3

Sandra was always considered a quiet girl. No one noticed her much at school. Even at home she didn't get as much attention as her brothers and sisters because she was well behaved and got along with everyone. Sandra didn't mind being the quiet one. She was used to it.

The music teacher was the first person to notice that Sandra had a beautiful voice. She started spending extra time with Sandra, teaching her singing technique. After a while, she asked Sandra to sing a solo in the chorus and then another. Pretty soon everyone at school had heard Sandra sing. They were all very impressed.

Suddenly, people began noticing her and Sandra blossomed. She not only showed people her voice, she let them see what a great sense of humor she had. Sandra was a lot of fun. She also had a lot of intelligent things to say. Once people began listening to her, they found she had a lot to offer. And once Sandra found her audience, she found she had a lot to say.

3A. What was Sandra like before she began to sing solo parts?

   A   She was outgoing.

   B   She was quiet.

   C   She was moody.

   D   She was funny.

3B. In what way did Sandra change?

_____

_____

_____

_____

_____

_____

SELECTION 4

Kyle and Leo were brothers. When people met them, they were always impressed with Kyle. He seemed to know all the answers to everything, and he let everybody know he knew. Whenever there was a discussion about anything, Kyle would always take the lead. Leo was quieter. You had the feeling he was watching what was going on. He didn't say much, but whenever he said something, it was well thought out. Most people didn't notice Leo. If you asked them, they would say that Kyle was the smartest, most accomplished of the brothers. They were sure he would be the most successful. But when it came to grades in school—and later, when they grew up, success in the world—Leo ended up doing much better.

4. How were Kyle and Leo different from each other?

   A   Kyle was much smarter and more successful than Leo.

   B   Leo was quieter about what he knew, but knew more.

   C   Leo was not as smart and didn't know as much as Kyle.

   D   Kyle didn't let on that he knew that much, but he did.

SELECTION 5

This selection comes from Mark Twain's story "Edward Mills and George Benton." It is about two orphaned cousins who are raised by Mr. and Mrs. Brant.

It was always sufficient to say, in answer to Eddie's petitions, "I would rather you would not do it"—meaning swimming, picnicking, berrying, circusing, and all sorts of things which boys delight in. But no answer was sufficient for Georgie; he had to be humored in his desires, or he would carry them with a high hand. Naturally, no boy got more swimming, skating, berrying, and so forth than he; no boy ever had a better time. The good Brants did not allow the boys to play out after nine in summer evenings; they were sent to bed at that hour; Eddie honorably remained, but Georgie usually slipped out of the window toward ten, and enjoyed himself till midnight.

5. Compare the two boys, based on the information in the selection.

   _____

   _____

   _____

   _____

   _____

   _____

PLOT AND SETTING

ANALYZING PLOTS

The **plot** of a story tells what happens. A plot may be simple or complicated. Here is an example of a very simple plot:

> Jan wanted a new bicycle. She asked her mother if she
> could get one, and her mother said yes.

No one would want to read this story. Readers want something more complex and interesting. In a good plot, things happen that create a **central problem** or **conflict**. The way the problem is worked out is called the resolution of the problem.

Read the next example. Notice how each event helps to develop the plot. What is the problem? How is it resolved?

EXAMPLE 1

Jerome and Morris were identical twins. Since very few people could tell them apart, they had fun fooling people. It had always been just a game, but one day it turned into a problem.

Jerome was absent from school. Morris told everyone he was Jerome. He pretended he was Jerome being a troublemaker. He was rude, he interrupted everyone, and he didn't do the work he was asked to do.

When Jerome came back to school, he found that everyone was angry with him. Knowing Morris, he thought he knew why. He didn't want people to think badly of him. From then on, Jerome dressed differently than Morris. He got a shorter haircut and made sure everyone knew which twin he was. If Morris wanted to make trouble, then he would be the one to get in trouble, too.

1. How did Jerome solve his problem?

    A He told everyone that his name was Morris.

    B He made himself look different from his twin.

    C He decided he would stay out of trouble.

    D He told everyone that Morris was the troublemaker.

B is the correct choice. Jerome solved the problem by making sure everyone knew which brother was which.

SETTING

The **setting** of a story is where and when it takes place. Sometimes the author describes the setting carefully. At other times, the author doesn't tell you the setting. You must figure it out for yourself.

Read the next example and decide where it takes place.

EXAMPLE 2

Toni wheeled her cart down the aisle. Because this aisle was much colder, she wished she had brought her sweater. Everything was behind glass doors. When she opened one of the doors to look inside, water condensed on the glass. Then when she closed it, she couldn't see through the door. There were many sizes and brands of ice cream. There were also a lot of flavors. Toni knew just what she wanted, mint chocolate chip. She found a carton of it and put it in her basket.

2. **Where was Toni?**

_____

_____

_____

_____

_____

_____

 Your teacher will discuss your answer.

STRATEGIES AND TIPS
FOR WORKING OUT A STORY'S PLOT AND SETTING

1   Try to identify the **central problem** or **conflict** in a passage. See if you can find the event that caused the problem.

2   Notice how the story ends. A story will often end with a **resolution** of its central problem.

3   Figure out where the story takes place. You may find that your own experiences and what you know about the world will help you decide this.

4   Look for clues that tell you when the story takes place. Are there clues that tell you the time of day, the time of the year, or a time in the past?

SELECTIONS FOR PRACTICE

SELECTION 1

Miguel came from a small town where everyone knew one another. They knew exactly what their neighbors were up to. Miguel didn't always like being watched so carefully, so he was happy to move to a big city.

When Miguel moved to the city, he did everything the same as he had when he lived in a small town. He rode his bicycle to the store and left it out front without locking it. In a small town someone would have seen his bike being stolen. In the city there were so many people around that no one knew it didn't belong to the thief.

The police returned his bike a few days later. It had been left in a park. Miguel realized that in a small town, people watch you and know your business. In a city you have to pay attention and watch yourself. Miguel learned that there were good things about living in a small town and good things about a big city.

1A. What problem did Miguel find in the city?

A   Things can be stolen.

B   People don't watch you.

C   It's much bigger.

D   He didn't make friends.

1B. What did he learn to do?

A   Make better friends.

B   Watch out for himself.

C   Not ride his bike.

D   Find his bike.

SELECTION 2

Donovan had to write a short story for homework. He couldn't come up with any ideas and besides, he didn't think he was much good at writing anyway. Somehow he kept finding other things to do. First he went to the refrigerator and got himself a snack. Then he remembered his mother wanted him to bring something down from the attic. That seemed like a good thing to do. The attic was full of interesting things. While he was in the attic, he came across a very old typewriter. He'd never seen anything like it before.

There was some paper next to the typewriter. Donovan decided to sit down at the desk that the typewriter was on. He put a sheet of paper in to see if the typewriter worked. He typed his name and the date. The keys were sticky but it was kind of fun to use. He liked the idea of working in the attic. He felt like a different person. He kept on typing. A short story idea came to him. He put in a clean sheet and began to write. When he finished, he found he had a pretty good story. He handed it in and his teacher liked it, too.

From then on, whenever Donovan had trouble writing, he went up to the attic and banged away at the old typewriter. Somehow it was more fun than writing a story by hand or on a computer. It must have been his lucky typewriter because he always ended up with something good.

2A. What was Donovan's problem?

A He didn't have anything to write with.

B He couldn't come up with any ideas.

C He had a lot of things to do around the house.

D He was very hungry and needed to eat.

2B. How did Donovan solve his problem?

_____

_____

_____

_____

_____

_____

SELECTION 3

It was a game, so Marisol was blindfolded. She had to guess where she was. It was, first of all, a very small space, too small to walk around in. If she stood up straight, she bumped into a wooden rod that went across the space. There were things hanging from the rod; one was warm, thick, and fluffy. Another was smooth and seemed to have long, arm-like things on each side. When Marisol took off her blindfold, it was so dark she couldn't see any better.

3. Where was Marisol?

    A In a bedroom.

    B In the kitchen.

    C In a closet.

    D In the basement.

SELECTION 4

There were trees all around, and the ground was covered with leaves of various colors. The ground was a rug of red, yellow, and brown hues. The trees were almost completely bare now. The pines were a dark, rich green. The air was brisk but not too cold.

4. What place and time of year does this passage describe?

   A   a park in the mid-summer

   B   a forest in late autumn

   C   a city street in the winter

   D   a neighborhood in early spring

SELECTION 5

In this selection from a story by Shirley Jackson, "Louisa, Please Come Home," the narrator is bothered by something on the radio.

"Louisa," my mother's voice came over the radio; it frightened me badly for a minute. "Louisa," she said, "please come home. It's been three long years since we saw you last; Louisa, I promise you that everything will be all right. We all miss you so. We want you back again. Louisa, please call home."

Once a year. On the anniversary of the day I ran away. Each time I heard it I was frightened again. . . .

5. Why is Louisa bothered by the radio message?

   A   She hates listening to the radio.

   B   Her mother doesn't really want to hear from her.

   C   She ran away from home, and her mother's message is a reminder.

   D   She has forgotten where she used to live.

SELECTION 6

As Gregor Samsa awoke one morning from uneasy dreams he found himself transformed in his bed into a gigantic insect. He was lying on his hard, as it were armor-plated, back and when he lifted his head a little he could see his dome-like brown belly divided into stiff arched segments on top of which the bed quilt could hardly keep in position and was about to slide off completely. His numerous legs, which were pitifully thin compared to the rest of his bulk, waved helplessly before his eyes.

—from "The Metamorphosis," by Franz Kafka

6. Gregor Samsa's main problem seems to be that he

   A had bad dreams.

   B is losing his bed quilt.

   C is no longer a human being.

   D has thin legs.

AUTHOR'S PURPOSE AND INTENDED AUDIENCE

AUTHOR'S PURPOSE

Books, stories, articles, and other pieces of writing are created for a variety of reasons. They may be written to entertain, to inform, to secure sympathy, or to prod the reader into action. They might be an opportunity for creating a mood or for the writer's self-expression.

Decide on the purpose of the following example.

EXAMPLE 1

Write your Congressional representative today and tell him you support the Jeffers-Hawkins bill. Without this bill, there will be no campaign spending reform. Candidates must be forced to change and limit their spending practices.

A phone call, letter, or e-mail to your representative in Congress can stop this abuse of power. Do it today, and make a difference.

1. This selection is intended to

    A inform readers.

    B prod readers to take action.

    C amuse readers.

    D sell a product to readers.

The correct answer is **B**. Although readers are informed, most of this selection seeks to get readers to do something. A discussion of campaign spending reform is plainly not meant to amuse readers, so choice C is wrong. And nothing is said about selling a product, so D is wrong as well.

INTENDED AUDIENCE

A selection may be written for children or adults, for scientists or sports fans. The **intended audience** for a selection is revealed by the language that the writer uses, by the topics covered, or by what the audience is assumed to know.

Read the next example and decide what audience it was written for:

EXAMPLE 2

As Tommy Jackson came flying around third base, he caught his foot on the bag and injured his knee. He'll be on the disabled list for a minimum of three weeks. Dominic Hoskins will replace him, and let's hope he can hit the curve ball better this time out.

2. This selection is written for

    A   medical doctors.

    B   kindergarten students.

    C   sports fans.

    D   police officers.

The correct answer is **C**. Choice D is not correct because nothing in the selection deals with police matters. The selection is too difficult for kindergarten students, and does not have enough medical information to be appropriate for doctors. The language and style suggest that it was written for sports fans.

Decide on the intended audience for the next example.

EXAMPLE 3

Thomas Egan, male, age 26, was admitted to the Orthopedic Center yesterday afternoon at 4:05 p.m. with an injury to the left knee sustained in the course of a baseball game. The admitting physician, Marta Ortesa, tentatively diagnosed the injury as a torn medial meniscus and directed the patient to the diagnostic center. Dr. Haworth recommended rest for one week and tentatively scheduled orthopedic surgery immediately after conclusion of the baseball season.

3. Was this selection written for a child or an adult? Use specific details from the selection in your answer.

_____

_____

_____

_____

_____

 Your teacher will discuss your answer.

STRATEGIES AND TIPS
FOR DETERMINING AUTHOR'S PURPOSE
AND INTENDED AUDIENCE

1 Read the passage and consider how it makes you feel. This may help you understand the **author's purpose**.

2 Where a selection was published provides a clue to its purpose. Newspaper editorials try to persuade. Textbooks are intended for instruction.

3 Nonfiction is usually written to inform. The writer may also be trying to instruct, persuade, or entertain readers.

4 Where a selection was published will probably help you decide whom it was written for.

5 Study the language used and the topic covered in the selection to decide what audience it was written for.

SELECTIONS FOR PRACTICE

SELECTION 1

The climate and building materials that are native to a region often influence the type of homes that are built there. When this country was first settled, trees were plentiful and most houses in the East were built of logs. In parts of the West, settlers built houses of adobe bricks because the area had a plentiful supply of clay and the climate was warm and dry. The bricks, made of a mixture clay and straw, harden and dry in the sun. The area gets little rainfall, so there is little chance that the bricks will fall apart.

Modern transportation has made it possible to ship building materials from one region to another. However, certain home designs in an area don't change, because the designs suit the climate. One-story, flat-topped houses are popular in warm climates. These houses have sliding glass doors and windows to let in sunlight and breezes. In regions where it snows often, flat-roofed houses are impractical because the weight of the snow could weaken and possibly collapse the roof. In such areas, homes have slanting roofs to let the snow slide off.

1. The purpose of this selection is to

   A   inform.

   B   persuade.

   C   entertain.

   D   sell products.

SELECTION 2

In general, it is a good idea for neighbors to help neighbors. In some communities there is something called a neighborhood watch. Other places call it a neighborhood alert. The people on those blocks look out for each other. If something suspicious happens on the block, a neighbor is often around to call the police. This discourages burglary. Some blocks have block parents. Then children on the block know where to go if they run into trouble and their parents are not around. In parts of the country where there is the danger of earthquakes, some neighborhoods have developed a system to account for everyone should a disaster happen. Whatever the need, the people who live closest to us can help us the most. We should begin working in our own community to develop a network of support within each neighborhood.

2. What is the purpose of this selection?

   A   to entertain

   B   to provide instructions

   C   to inform and persuade

   D   to create a mood

SELECTION 3

Introduce students to the more complex aspects of grammar by providing numerous examples. Do not introduce advanced terms and concepts until each of the preliminary terms has been carefully developed, tested, and reviewed.

3. This was written for

   A   economists.

   B   fifth-grade students.

   C   politicians.

   D   English teachers.

SELECTION 4

Test animals should not be fed for approximately 24 hours before the study. Body weight should be reduced at least 15%. Salt deprivation should be avoided by providing constant free access to salt sticks.

4. This selection would probably be found in a cookbook. Explain why you agree or disagree with this statement.

_____

_____

_____

_____

_____

_____

SELECTION 5

Dearest Meg,

I think only of you. When I wake in the morning, my thoughts are of you. When I eat breakfast, I wonder what you're eating in the morning. Your departure has left me sick with loneliness. Even though you will only be gone six days, I can't wait for you to come back. Tell me what train you'll take, and I'll meet you at the station.

5. This is a selection from a
   A love letter.
   B business letter.
   C school report.
   D work report.

UNDERSTANDING GRAPHIC ORGANIZERS

Tests sometimes ask you to complete **graphic organizers**. Graphic organizers help you to understand what you read. They consist of boxes or circles in charts or with lines connecting them. In this chapter, you will learn to use the most popular kinds of graphic organizers.

SEQUENCE

Read this passage and then see how the parts fit into a graphic organizer.

Loretta drove her car up to the pump. Prices had gone up nearly twenty cents a gallon. She prepaid with her credit card. She chose premium, which was always more expensive. She stuck the nozzle in her tank and filled it up. When she was done, she washed her windows and checked under the hood. She remembered to see how much air was in the tires. Everything was all right. Then she drove off.

Each box contains an event. These events are arranged in the **sequence** in which they occurred, with the earliest event at the left and the latest event on the right.

The next example also deals with sequence. Read the passage about starting a fire in a fireplace, and then look at the graphic organizer. It contains five boxes; one of them is empty. Decide which event belongs in the empty box.

EXAMPLE 1

Bring in enough wood for the fire. Make sure the wood is dry. Then check the fireplace and open the damper. Crumple up some pieces of newspaper. Before lighting the paper, put small dry sticks on top of it. When the sticks are burning, add a small log. If you leave the fire, put a fireplace screen in place.

1. Which words belong in the empty box?

- **A**   Crumple up newspaper
- **B**   Put screen in place
- **C**   Add a small log
- **D**   Bring wood in

The missing step is choice **A**, "Crumple up newspaper." This belongs in the empty box.

Here is the completed graphic:

TOPIC AND STORY DETAIL: WHEEL-TYPE GRAPHIC OR WEBBING

Another popular kind of graphic organizer consists of a circle surrounded by other circles. The circle in the middle contains a topic, and the other circles provide details about the topic. This kind of graphic organizer—called a **wheel-type graphic** or **webbing**—is used in the next example.

EXAMPLE 2

One of the most valuable substances in the world—the diamond—is also the hardest substance. Most people think of diamonds only as jewels used in rings, especially engagement rings; however, jewelry is only one of the uses for diamonds. Diamonds are also valuable to industry because they are much harder than any other substance and are excellent for cutting and drilling. Diamonds are also used for mechanical parts, which rub together, because diamonds don't wear down so quickly as other materials.

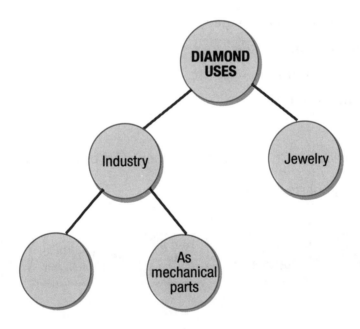

This passage is about diamonds and how they are used, so the words "Diamond uses" belong in the central circle. There are two circles connected to the "Diamond uses" circle. One says "Industry," and the other says "Jewelry." Two circles are connected to the "Industry" circle. One says "As mechanical parts." The other is empty.

2. **What detail belongs in the empty box?**

   A   for cutting and drilling

   B   for engagement rings

   C   hard

   D   valuable

 Your teacher will discuss your answer.

COMPARISON: TWO-COLUMN CHARTS OR T-CHARTS

Graphic organizers can be very helpful when you are comparing people, things, or ideas. For example, a simple two-column chart (also called a T-chart) may be used to compare things.

Suppose that you were asked to compare a pencil with a pen. You could draw two columns like the ones below. You would decide how a pencil differs from a pen and then write these differences in the two columns.

Pencil	Pen
Wood	Plastic
Graphite	Ink
Erasable	Permanent

In the next example, you will read about the differences between Rashan and Charles. Then you will see a chart that lists their differences. Your task will be to complete this chart.

EXAMPLE 3

Rashan and Charles were cousins, both of them born at noon on the same day, three thousand miles apart. They were both very good at doing most things. They were excellent basketball players, did well in school, and were both well liked. Rashan was running for class president. The year before, he had been class treasurer. The year before that he was on the Student Government Board. He always tried to achieve as much as possible. It was the same with him in sports. Everybody likes to win, but Rashan didn't let down for a minute. He gave it his all. He wanted to score the most points.

Charles did everything well too, but it didn't matter to him if he came in first. He had no desire to hold any kind of class office. He was happy to just be there and help out. In sports he was a real team player. Everyone liked having his support, but he never tried to make any flashy moves.

Rashan	Charles
Wanted to win	Didn't care about winning
Running for president	Didn't want to hold office
Tried to score the most points	

3.   What detail belongs in the empty space?

A   team player

B   on Student Government Board

C   gave everything his all

D   class treasurer

Choice **A** is correct—Charles, not Rashan, was a team player. The other choices describe Rashan.

COMPARISON: VENN DIAGRAMS

In the last example, you completed a two-column chart that listed ways that Rashan and Charles were different. Sometimes you will be asked how two things are the **same** as well as how they are **different**. Another kind of graphic organizer can be used to show how people or things differ and how they are the same. It is called a **Venn diagram**. The Venn diagram below shows how Rashan and Charles are different and how they are alike.

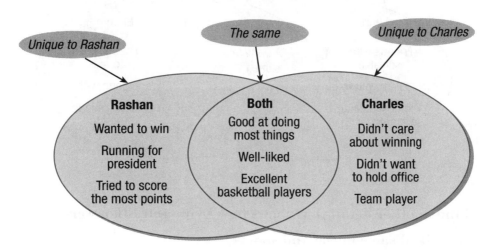

Notice that this kind of diagram is made up of two overlapping circles.

❖ In the parts of the circles that **don't overlap**, you list the **differences** between Rashan and Charles.

❖ In the **overlapping** part, you list the things they have **in common**.

Read this passage about Lynn and Ellen. Then study the Venn diagram that shows how the two differed and how they were similar. Complete the diagram by finding something else the two had in common.

EXAMPLE 4

Lynn was a few hours older than her twin sister, Ellen. They looked so much alike that people confused each for the other. You would have thought Lynn was five years older. She was always telling Ellen what to do. She seemed to think she knew best, and she didn't like being disagreed with.

Lynn was lucky to have a sister like Ellen. Ellen was willing to go along with almost everything Lynn suggested. For one thing, they liked the same music and sports. They liked the same movies too. But their tastes in friends was very different. Ellen liked people who read a lot. Lynn liked people who were sociable.

Ellen didn't like to argue or make waves, so most of the time the twins spent time with Lynn's friends. Ellen liked having Lynn there to help her decide what to do.

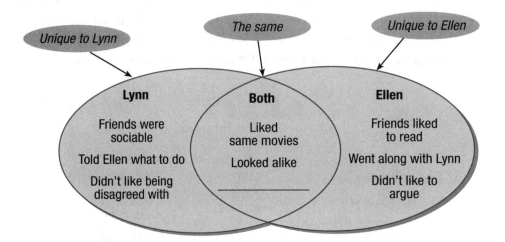

4. Find another detail that shows how Lynn and Ellen were similar.

   A   liked same music and sports

   B   spent time with Ellen's friends

   C   liked having the other make decisions

   D   enjoyed arguing

 Your teacher will discuss your answer.

BOX CHARTS

Another kind of chart consists of a set of boxes. By filling in the empty boxes, you can show the main points of a story or article.

EXAMPLE 5

Serendipity means a discovery that starts with a bit of luck. Throughout history, there have been many examples of this type of breakthrough.

For instance, until the 1830s, rubber wasn't used much. Tires and rubber boats could never have been made out of the raw rubber available then. Charles Goodyear was an inventor who was trying to make rubber that would work better. Goodyear wasn't a trained chemist, had lost his money in bad business investments, and had just been released from prison because of money he owed. He was hoping to make a fortune and get out of debt by making better rubber, but his experiments weren't working. One day he spilled some of his mixture on a hot stove. When he got it off the stove, he found he had finally made rubber that could be used.

On another occasion, a German chemist was doing experiments in his house in 1845. He had promised his wife he wouldn't do any such work at home, but she was away, so he decided he'd do a little experimental research. He was working with powerful acids and accidentally spilled some of the mixture. He was afraid it would damage the table, so he grabbed his wife's cotton apron and wiped up the acids. Then he hung the apron on the stove to dry. It exploded. The mixture of cotton with the two acids produced guncotton, which became an important explosive.

The discovery of penicillin, one the most important drugs ever produced, also began with a lucky discovery. Sir Alexander Fleming noticed that a bit of mold got into one of his experimental cultures, probably because it was blown into an uncovered dish by the air. The green mold killed the disease-causing bacteria that grew in the dish. Fleming was lucky. He was not only lucky but also intelligent. He didn't ignore his finding. He went on to prove that the mold killed the deadly bacteria. His work was the first step in developing the wonder drug penicillin. Many of us owe our lives to Fleming and the scientists who followed up on his discovery. It took a long time before penicillin was produced from the mold.

Serendipity helps, but hard work is also necessary.

Invention	Discovery	Accident
Useful rubber	heating the mixture	spilled on stove
Guncotton	mixing cotton with acids	
Penicillin	a mold that killed bacteria	a mold blew onto a culture

5. What belongs in the empty space?

    A   being released from prison

    B   wiping up a spill

    C   damaging the table

    D   making a promise to his wife

The selection says that the chemist discovered guncotton after wiping up a spill with his wife's apron. So the correct choice is **B**.

STRATEGIES AND TIPS
FOR USING GRAPHIC ORGANIZERS

1   To complete a **graphic organizer**, fill in the empty box or circle by picking the correct answer choice.

2   To complete a **sequence graphic**, read what's inside the boxes on either side of the empty box. Then check the selection. Ask yourself which event in the selection occurs between the event in the box *before* the empty box and the event in the box *after* the empty box.

3   In a **web**, the main idea goes in the center circle. The supporting details are arranged in circles that surround the circle in the center.

4   Graphic organizers that ask you to compare events, settings, or characters are usually arranged in columns. Each column is headed by the name of a person, place, or event. You must find details that belong with that name.

5   **Venn diagrams** have two overlapping circles. The outside parts of the circles show differences. The inside part shows what both topics have in common.

SELECTIONS FOR PRACTICE

SELECTION 1

When Lisa was born, she got all her parents' attention. She was an only child. When she first learned to walk and talk, her parents acted as though she were a genius. Every picture she made was a work of art; every song she sang was beautiful. Lisa was very proud of herself. But she thought she was better than everyone else. Lisa began to brag a lot.

Then Lisa's mother had another daughter, Peggy. Suddenly Lisa wasn't the center of all the attention. Peggy seemed just as wonderful as Lisa seemed before. Her parents told all their friends how special Peggy was. Lisa started to think that maybe she wasn't so great after all.

One day she was feeling sad and ignored. She squeezed into a large wastepaper container and sat down. Her mother found her there. "Whatever are you doing?" she asked her daughter.

"You don't need me anymore now that you have Peggy. This is where something that you don't need goes."

Her mother pulled her out of the container and hugged her hard. "You are very special to us," she said. "Both you and Peggy are special. I guess I've been spending too little time with you."

Then Lisa smiled. After that she felt better.

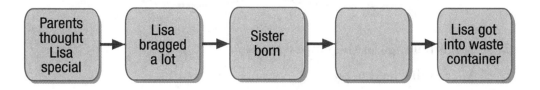

1. According to the information in the passage, what belongs in the empty box?

    A   Lisa smiled.

    B   Lisa's mother hugged her.

    C   Lisa felt ignored.

    D   Lisa got all the attention.

SELECTION 2

Denise lived in Los Angeles and Phyllis lived in Chicago. They became pen pals over the Internet and learned a lot about each other by exchanging e-mail. The first thing they learned about each other was that one of them wrote much more often than the other.

Phyllis wrote long, chatty mail, which she only sent once a month. Denise liked to write almost every day, like a diary entry. She would just write one or two lines saying what was happening with her. She might describe the weather or her mood. She had lots of moods because little things affected her. If a flower outside her window wilted, she might describe it sadly. On a bright sunny day, her mood was lifted and she would sound as if she had won the lottery.

Phyllis was almost always sunny, and her letters were sunny, too. She babbled on and on about how great things were and what fun she was having. It made Denise very happy to hear from Phyllis.

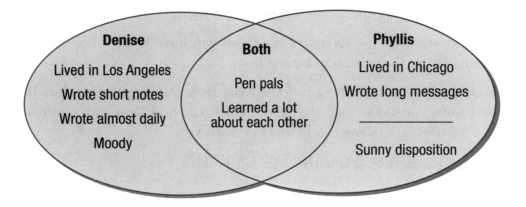

2. What belongs in the empty space?

   A   exchanged e-mail

   B   either sad or happy

   C   wrote messages like diary entries

   D   wrote once a month

SELECTION 3

A caricature is a drawing that exaggerates a person's expressions and features to make fun of the person. If, for example, an artist wants to make fun of a person with a long nose, the caricature will show the person's nose two or three times longer than it really is.

When caricatures were first drawn, about 500 years ago, they were not funny. Rather, they were frightening pictures that were very popular in those days—pictures of devils and skeletons. Later, when Dutch and English artists began to draw caricatures of famous people in politics, business, and society, the pictures showed the silly, humorous side of these people. Other drawings poked fun at the customs of the time. These caricatures were a lot like the political cartoons we have today in newspapers. Present-day caricatures make fun of the president of the United States or a senator or some other figure of national importance.

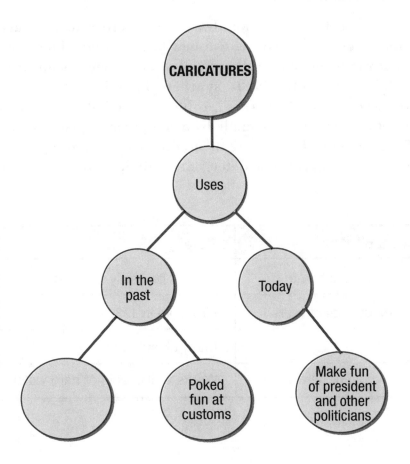

3. What goes in the empty circle?

   A   long noses

   B   frightening pictures

   C   Dutch and English artists

   D   newspapers

SELECTION 4

For thousands of years, people have been using soaps made from natural ingredients like animal fats and vegetable fats. Even today, bath and hand soaps are made from these same ingredients. Natural soaps, however, have always had one drawback. In cold water or in hard water (water in which there is an unusually large amount of minerals), natural soaps do not make suds easily. The soap and the minerals combine instead to form soap curd, a substance which is not useful for cleaning. In fact, soap curd itself is a cleaning problem, because it causes bathtub rings.

Because natural soap was not always an effective cleaning agent, soap manufacturers tried to develop a new kind of soap. They wanted a new soap that would clean as well in hard or cold water as natural soaps did in soft, hot water. In the 1930s, synthetic household detergents, the solution to the soap manufacturers' problem, were put on the market. These synthetic detergents are made by a complicated process from many different chemicals—among them, fats, coal tar, and petroleum. Unlike natural soaps, synthetic detergents cannot easily be made in the home.

Natural Soap	Detergent
Can be made in the home	Cannot be easily made at home
Made for thousands of years	First sold in 1930s
	Many chemicals
Problems in cold or hard water	Works well in cold or hard water

4. What belongs in the empty box?

    A   Soap curd

    B   Coal tar and petroleum

    C   Synthetic

    D   Natural ingredients

SELECTION 5

Few of us can imagine life before the development of readily available electricity. The modern home would be without light, telephone, radio, television, and portable heating units. Prior to electricity, life was substantially more limited. Reading at night by candlelight or gaslight was difficult at best, as were many other activities we now take for granted. Many valuable work hours were lost because of the lack of light. People were more bound by the constraints of sunlight, more limited in available activities, and more isolated because of the difficulties of communication.

	Before Electricity	After Electricity
Reliance on sunlight	more	less
Activities		less limited
Telephone, radio, television	none	many

5. What belongs in the empty box?

    A   more limited

    B   gaslight and candlelight

    C   work hours

    D   greater opportunities

10

FACT VS. OPINION

A **fact** can be checked. Somebody can determine whether it is true. For example, if a car dealer states that a car has been driven 60,102 miles, anyone can check the odometer and discover whether the statement is true.

An **opinion**, on the other hand, depends on a person's judgment. If you say that soccer is a lot of fun to watch, that is your opinion.

Read the next selection. Assume that each statement is accurate. Then answer the question about fact and opinion.

EXAMPLE 1

Johnny Hilltop, the greatest star today, is 6'4". He's the most talented actor in the country and has the cutest smile.

1.   Which of these statements is NOT an opinion?

   A   Johnny is 6'4".

   B   He is the most talented actor.

   C   He has the cutest smile.

   D   He is the greatest star.

It is possible to check height. The statement that Johnny is 6'4" is a fact. The other statements are matters of opinion, not fact.

Now read this example and decide which statement IS an opinion, not a fact.

EXAMPLE 2

"Give me liberty or give me death!" Patrick Henry, an American patriot, spoke these words over two hundred years ago. In the 1760s, when Patrick Henry began his speech making, America was ruled by England. Some American colonists were beginning to feel that England was making severe and unjust laws for its American colonies, and others, even more angry, thought that England had no right to rule the American colonies. Patrick Henry was one of the first people to publicly argue for greater freedom for the colonies. His speeches were so powerful that he was the greatest orator of his time.

In his most famous speech, Henry was hoping to convince the colonists in his home colony of Virginia to prepare for war with England. At that time, some Americans felt that the colonies should try to improve relations with England because, in the event of war, the Americans would be so outnumbered that they would be crushed by England's army. Speaking to these people who wanted to avoid war, Patrick Henry said: "Is life so dear, or peace so sweet, as to be purchased at the price of chains and slavery? Forbid it, Almighty God! I know not what course others may take, but as for me, give me liberty or give me death!"

2A. Which statement expresses an opinion?

A Patrick Henry was one of the first people to publicly argue for greater freedom for the colonies.

B His speeches were so powerful that he was the greatest orator of his time.

C In his most famous speech, Henry was hoping to convince the colonists in his home colony of Virginia to prepare for war with England.

D At that time, some Americans felt that the colonies should try to improve relations with England.

2B. Find a statement of fact in the passage. How can you tell that it is a fact?

_____

_____

_____

_____

_____

_____

Your teacher will discuss your answers.

STRATEGIES AND TIPS
FOR DETERMINING FACT AND OPINION

1 If a statement can be checked or proven, it is a **fact**.

2 If a statement expresses someone's personal judgment or feelings, it is an **opinion**.

3 Words like *think*, *feel*, and *believe* are clues that a statement is an opinion.

SELECTIONS FOR PRACTICE

SELECTION 1

When Donna dances, she always looks like a gawky bird. She isn't very good at singing, either. I don't think she deserved it, but she won first prize in the last talent contest.

1. Which part of the selection states a fact?
   A   She looks like a gawky bird when she dances.
   B   She isn't good at singing.
   C   I don't think she deserved the prize.
   D   She won first prize in the last talent contest.

SELECTION 2

Jack will make a poor pilot. He's shorter than the Air Force regulations permit. He also has gotten sick to his stomach every time he has been in a plane. And he forgot to take the most recent test for his license.

2. Which statement is an opinion?

A   Jack will make a poor pilot.

B   He's shorter than the Air Force regulations permit.

C   He also has gotten sick to his stomach every time he has been in a plane.

D   He forgot to take the most recent test for his license.

SELECTION 3

Starfish are among the most widespread of marine animals. In spite of their name, starfish are not really fish at all since they are invertebrates and do not have backbones. Starfish come in many colors and usually have five arms, or rays. When starfish are dried out, they make attractive ornaments and necklaces.

3. Which sentence contains an opinion?

A   Starfish are among the most widespread of marine animals.

B   In spite of their name, starfish are not really fish at all, since they are invertebrates and do not have backbones.

C   Starfish come in many colors and usually have five arms, or rays.

D   When starfish are dried out, they make attractive ornaments and necklaces.

SELECTION 4

It is hard not to be impressed by the latest addition to our literary community. Emil Potter is in every sense of the word a true Renaissance man. His latest novella smacks of an incredible grasp of philosophical concepts. His prose is bountiful and his insights, stunning. It is a pleasure to know that last Tuesday he joined our small society. Ladies and Gentlemen, I give you Emil Potter.

4. Write one fact from the passage. Explain why it is a fact.

    _____

    _____

    _____

    _____

    _____

    _____

SELECTION 5

As many times as I have tried to train my dog not to jump on people, she persists in this habit. I have gone to dog training lessons and learned all the commands. The trainer worked with her over and over, trying to break her of this one trait. The last time my boss came over to visit, my dog nearly knocked him down. Needless to say, he didn't seem very pleased with either me or the dog. She is a wonderful dog, but she makes my life very difficult.

5. Which statement contains an opinion?

    A The dog jumps on people.

    B I have gone to dog-training lessons.

    C The dog nearly knocked my boss over.

    D The dog is wonderful.

SELECTION 6

As a kid, Ernest started playing football with the other youngsters on his block. They would all walk down to the empty field at the other side of town to play. Ernest was the smallest in the group and was always considered a liability. No one ever wanted to pick him, so he was always last to be chosen, which caused him endless embarrassment. Now that Ernest was first-string quarterback at State, he could look back on his pain philosophically. Perhaps all those difficult years had made him a better person, less contemptuous of those players who weren't gifted. Today he would be playing the final game of the season and, if State won, it would mean the championship title. Although usually he was very nervous before a ball game, today he felt very calm. In an hour he would go the athletic building and change for the game. If he took this one, his career would be made. He would obviously get the offer he wanted from the pros. He wondered what all his friends back in Moodus would think of that—little Ernie a big star.

6. Which statement is an opinion?

   A   Ernest was the smallest in the group.

   B   Ernest was a liability.

   C   Ernest was first-string quarterback at State.

   D   Ernest was last to be chosen for a team.

11

INFERENCES AND PREDICTIONS

Questions based on a reading selection may ask you to make **inferences**—to reach conclusions based on the information in the selection. In this chapter we will look at two kinds of inference questions: drawing conclusions and predicting outcomes.

DRAWING CONCLUSIONS

In your life and in your reading, you continually **draw conclusions** based on whatever information you have. For example, if a man enters your house through the window and comes out carrying a television set that looks like yours, you will draw the conclusion that he is a thief. There may be another explanation for the man's action, but on the basis of what you have seen so far, concluding that he is a thief seems like the best bet.

Read the following example about unicorns and draw a conclusion based on what you read.

EXAMPLE 1

Intertwined throughout the legends of the Middle Ages are fantastic accounts of a purely mythical animal, the unicorn. In these legends the unicorn is depicted as a beautiful, graceful animal with the head and body of a horse, the tail of a lion, and the quick, strong legs of an antelope. But the distinguishing feature of the unicorn was the sharp, spiraled horn that supposedly protruded from the middle of its forehead.

NOTICE: Photocopying any part of this book is forbidden by law.

1. From this passage, it is clear that unicorns

    A   existed only during the Middle Ages.

    B   never existed.

    C   were valuable to their owners.

    D   were stronger than other animals.

The correct answer is **B**. Since the passage refers to "legends," "fantastic accounts," and "a purely mythical animal," it is correct to draw the conclusion that unicorns never existed.

PREDICTING OUTCOMES

We can often make reasonable predictions on the basis of what we know from the past. A football star who has averaged two touchdowns a game is likely to score again the next time out. An A student will probably do well on the next exam. A man who dresses well will probably look good the next time you see him. In all of these cases we cannot be sure, but we are able to predict the outcome with reasonable accuracy on the basis of what we know.

EXAMPLE 2

Angus and Martha Davis never had the children they wanted. It was a shame because they were natural-born parents. They loved children, they were kind and generous, and they were very wise. They never considered adoption until they saw a television program about orphans in Romania. They felt moved by the sad conditions that these children lived in. They decided to take one of them into their home. It worked out very well for the Davises and the little girl they adopted. One child didn't seem like enough, and so when they heard of a child from Central America that needed a home, they were happy to provide one for him.

The Davis household was a cheerful, warm, and safe environment for these displaced children from different parts of the world. Soon there were five adopted children filling the rooms of their modest home.

On the news one evening, Angus Davis saw a segment about the children of the former Yugoslavia. Many children there had been left without a home or family because of war.

2. **What do you think happened next?**

_____

_____

_____

_____

_____

_____

 Your teacher will discuss your answer.

STRATEGIES AND TIPS
FOR MAKING INFERENCES

1 When you are asked to make an **inference**, read over the passage and make a decision. The answer will NOT be found directly in the passage.

2 **Draw a conclusion** or **predict an outcome** based on the facts in the passage.

3 Look at the answer choices. Decide which choice is the closest to your own conclusion or prediction.

SELECTIONS FOR PRACTICE

SELECTION 1

School elections were coming up. Tanya was running for class president against Marilyn. Everyone knew Marilyn and everyone liked her. She had always lived in that neighborhood. She thought she had it made. Tanya was new and didn't know as many people. She was a hard worker and would do a lot for the school but didn't seem to have as much going for her. Then they counted the ballots. Tanya won. She was surprised and thrilled. Marilyn was surprised as well.

1. Why was Marilyn surprised?

   A She thought that Tanya was the better person for the job.

   B She expected to win because she was better known.

   C She thought Tanya wasn't as nice a person.

   D She didn't expect to win.

SELECTION 2

Many blind people are accompanied everywhere they go by harnessed German shepherd dogs. These dogs are not pets, but guide dogs that are trained in special schools located throughout the United States and other countries.

The Germans were the first to develop programs to train guide dogs. That is why, even today, most guide dogs, or Seeing Eye dogs as they are called in the United States, are German shepherds. Female German shepherds usually are chosen, although boxers or retrievers sometimes are used. In the Seeing Eye school, the dogs learn to obey spoken commands and to respond to signals given through the special harnesses the dogs wear around their chests. The training is done by professional trainers, and the entire training program takes about three months. At the end of the program, the dog's new owner comes to the school and spends about a month there getting used to his new dog. The blind owner and the dog practice all the commands the dog has learned during its three-month training program.

2.   Why is the guide dog's harness important?

   A   Most guide dogs are not well trained, and the harness keeps the dog from running away.

   B   A blind person gives the dog signals through the harness.

   C   The harness protects the dog from the cold and rain.

   D   The Germans were the first people to train guide dogs.

SELECTION 3

The Johnston family had a new puppy. It had an insatiable appetite. It would eat everything in sight. No one could leave the table without having someone stand guard over the food. Otherwise, the puppy would down whatever food was left behind. One time, Mattie Johnston left a roast on the table and went to call everyone to dinner. When they walked in to eat, they found the puppy on a chair, about to climb onto the table. They saved the roast just in time.

3.   A platter of leftover turkey and stuffing was sitting unattended on the Johnston's dinner table for an hour. What do you think happened?

   _____

   _____

   _____

   _____

   _____

   _____

SELECTION 4

Tony, the school's prize athlete, was worried. He wanted desperately to go on to college and study medicine, but his teacher told him that the only way he would ever get into college was by working much harder and raising his grades. Despite his great love of sports, Tony reluctantly stopped playing football, cut down on basketball, and went home every afternoon to study. His parents were amazed by his commitment. He even cut out going camping with his friends that fall, because there was a big science exam coming up.

He had always looked down at students who turned in long reports and spent long hours in the library, but now he started to do it himself. In less than three months his grades began to climb, and by the end of the semester he was an honors student. Although he missed playing sports—particularly football—as much as he did before, he felt that doing well in school was more important.

4. What would probably happen if Tony needed to get a job?

    A   He would look for a job at first but then join the football team instead.

    B   He would ask his dad to find him a job.

    C   He would would look hard and wouldn't quit until he was hired.

    D   He would wait until someone came to his door and offered him a job.

SELECTION 5

Some scientists think that the North American Indians are descended from wandering Asian tribes that crossed to North America; perhaps they made the crossing by a land bridge in the far north. Some of these Indians went to Mexico. The early Indians living in northern Mexico remained primitive wanderers; however, the Indians of central and southern Mexico gave up their nomadic life as hunters and warriors. Many of these tribes lived in cities, around which they planted large fields of corn and vegetables.

The most highly developed of these Indian cultures grew up in the Valley of Mexico. Forests and fertile land encircled a large lake in the middle of this valley, which was surrounded by high mountains. In this ideal setting, an early tribe built Teotihuacán, a city of pyramids and palaces. Later, the Toltecs came and built a more developed city in this Valley of Mexico. Finally, the Aztec-Mexica tribe came to the valley and built Tenochtitlan, a beautiful city on an island in the middle of the lake. Three bridges connected the island to the mainland. The Spanish conquered the city in 1521 and renamed it Mexico City, after the Aztec-Mexica tribe they had conquered.

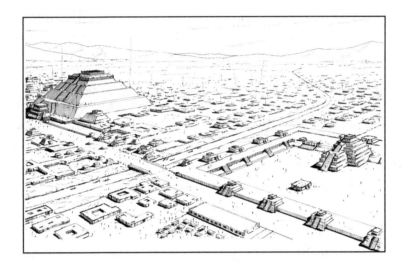

5. According to the information in this selection, Mexico City

A   has ties to ancient civilizations.

B   was always a Spanish city.

C   was home to nomads.

D   was on top of a mountain.

12

COMPARISONS

An author often makes a concept clear by showing how it is **similar to** or **different from** another concept. For example, we can understand the French Revolution better if we study how it was similar to the American Revolution and how it differed from the American Revolution. Similarly, we can understand an ape's ability to use language by seeing how its skills are similar to those of a human child. At the same time, we can understand its limitations by seeing how its capabilities differ from those of an adult.

LIKENESS OR SIMILARITY

Common terms indicating likenesses are: *same*, *both*, *similarly*, *as well as*, *another*, *likewise*, *for example*. Notice how comparisons are made in the following example.

EXAMPLE 1

Early in the evening, a pond may be filled with the sound of frogs making their low-pitched croaking sounds. All the sounds come from the male frog; the female is silent. The male croak or song enables the female to select a mate and then to find him. Song has the same function in the bird kingdom. The female chooses a male bird by his song and then uses the sound to locate him.

1. According to the selection, which sex produces the call or song?
    A   Male frogs and male birds.
    B   Male frogs and female birds.
    C   Female frogs and female birds.
    D   Female frogs and male birds.

The correct choice is **A**, *Male frogs and male birds*. The selection states that song functions the same way in the bird kingdom as with frogs. *Both* male frogs and male birds use song in the *same* way.

DIFFERENCE OR CONTRAST

Key words that indicate difference or contrast include: *however, on the other hand, but, unlike, in contrast to, as contrasted to.* In the next example, notice how difference is indicated.

EXAMPLE 2

Of the two major kinds of destructive storms, tornadoes usually begin over land. On the other hand, hurricanes almost never begin like tornadoes.

2A. Based on the example, which statement is most likely?

   A   Tornadoes and hurricanes begin over land.

   B   Tornadoes and hurricanes begin over water.

   C   Tornadoes begin over land; hurricanes, over water.

   D   Hurricanes begin like tornadoes.

The correct choice is **C**. Although the example does not tell where hurricanes begin, we know they do not begin over land.

2B. What point of similarity between tornadoes and hurricanes does the passage mention?

_____

_____

_____

_____

_____

_____

 Your teacher will discuss your answer.

NOTICE: Photocopying any part of this book is forbidden by law.

STRATEGIES AND TIPS
FOR MAKING COMPARISONS

1 Look for key words that introduce similarities and differences between two ideas, persons, or things.

2 Note whether the two items being compared are similar, different, or a combination of similarities and differences.

3 It is sometimes helpful to compare two items by listing similarities and differences in a chart.

SELECTIONS FOR PRACTICE

SELECTION 1

When television was first invented, many people feared it would mark an end to reading, that people would prefer to sit in front of television rather than read either books or newspapers. Contrary to this popular opinion, today there are more books and other printed material published and sold than ever before.

1. According to the selection, how much do people read now as compared to the period before television?

   A People read less than they used to.

   B People today read more than they used to.

   C People read about the same as they used to.

   D The selection does not help us answer this question.

SELECTION 2

Butterflies and moths look very much alike. The best way to tell them apart is to look at their antennae. Butterfly antennae are slender and the ends are rounded into little knobs, while moth antennae lack these knobs.

Most butterflies fly and feed during the daytime and rest in the night. When they rest, butterflies have their wings upright over their backs. Butterflies feed on the nectar of flowers and on other plant liquids. A long slender sucking tube acts as the insect's mouth. The butterfly probes deep into the plant and sucks up the nectar.

Both moths and butterflies go through a life cycle that involves a substantial change called metamorphosis. The female lays many eggs from which caterpillars hatch. The caterpillar devours plants, turns into a pupa, and finally becomes a butterfly or moth.

2. How are butterflies and moths similar?

_____

_____

_____

_____

_____

_____

SELECTION 3

Diseases travel at the same rate that people do. When it took people three days to travel from one town to another, it took a disease the same time to get there. Today with jet travel, we must be prepared to deal with the immediate spread of illness. A flu-causing virus may begin in China and spread to Australia within a few days.

3. Compared to the 17th century, diseases today spread

    A   more slowly than they used to.

    B   at about the same speed as they used to.

    C   more rapidly than they used to.

    D   none of the above.

SELECTION 4

After years of poorly rewarded labor, Chester Carlson made a fortune from the invention of the copying machine. This single idea earned more than $100 million for the inventor. Even simple concepts like the design of the safety pin or the eraser on the end of a pencil made their inventors rich. In contrast to these well-rewarded ideas, the efforts of most inventors have received neither financial nor personal recognition.

4. According to the selection, which is true?

    A   The safety pin injured more people than it helped.

    B   The invention of the safety pin brought the inventor riches, but most inventions were financially unrewarding.

    C   Most inventors got rich; the inventor of the pencil with an eraser did not get rich.

    D   Neither the inventor of the copy machine nor most other inventors get rich.

SELECTION 5

Anyone who knew Robert was surprised to find out that Ian was his brother. Ian wanted to be in show business. He was always fun to be around, cracking jokes or making a game out of everything. When Ian walked into a room, you always knew he was there. His booming laugh could be heard from anywhere around him. In the lunchroom at school, on the school grounds after school, wherever he was, a small crowd was always gathered around him.

Robert was rarely with more than one other person. Usually when he spent time with a friend, they'd just talk. Sometimes they would take something apart to see how it worked or they would build things together. Most often, Robert liked to be alone. It was easier to do the things he liked to do by himself.

5. How did Ian and Robert differ?

   A   Robert was smarter and nicer than Ian.

   B   Ian was a people person and Robert was more of a loner.

   C   Ian was good at mechanical things and Robert wasn't.

   D   Robert was a good actor and Ian was more scientific.

13

PARAGRAPH DEVELOPMENT AND LOGICAL ORDER

LOGICAL ORDER

There are many ways to **organize** a paragraph or a longer selection. For example, a writer may begin an explanation of how cars work by starting with the front of the car and working to the back. Or the writer may start with the engine and then discuss the electrical system and the brake system. Perhaps the writer will start with earlier models of cars and move on toward a discussion of present-day models. The writer may choose any form of organization, as long as it is logical and clear to the reader.

In order to make the order clear to the reader, a writer often uses key words like *first* or *last*. These words are also called **transition words**.

Read the three sentences below and decide how they should be ordered in a paragraph. To help you determine the correct order, pay attention to the transition words *later* and *finally*.

EXAMPLE 1

    A Finally, as a leading general, MacArthur commanded large armies.

    B In his early years, MacArthur was the best student at West Point.

    C Later, he was a brave and successful young officer.

1. **Which would be the correct order of these sentences in a paragraph?**

   A A B C

   B B A C

   C B C A

   D C B A

The correct choice is **BCA**. The word *finally* shows that sentence A comes last. The word *later* shows that sentence C comes after sentence B. And, of course, the phrase *early years* in sentence B indicates that it probably comes first.

Such transition terms as *first*, *second*, *last*, *originally*, *subsequently*, *early years*, and *later years* indicate a logical order organized by **time**. Terms like *bottom*, *middle*, and *top* might indicate a logical order organized by **space**.

Choose the correct order in the next example.

EXAMPLE 2

   A The folder for each physician goes in the middle.

   B The blue forms go on the right.

   C Place the yellow cards with the patient's name on the left.

2. **To place these sentences so they give instructions in left-to-right order, they should be written**

   A C A B

   B B A C

   C C B A

   D A B C

 Your teacher will discuss your answer.

Sometimes logical order will be determined by the natural flow of thought from one idea to another. Decide the proper order for these sentences.

EXAMPLE 3

A Learning how to swim is one of the most natural things in the world.

B They think they will drown if they even get their heads wet.

C But surprisingly, some people are terrified of trying.

3. Which is the correct order?

A A B C

B C B A

C B A C

D A C B

Sentence C follows sentence A logically. Then sentence B follows sentence A. The correct order is therefore **ACB**.

STRATEGIES AND TIPS
FOR UNDERSTANDING PARAGRAPH DEVELOPMENT AND LOGICAL ORDER

1 Items in a paragraph should be in correct, logical order.

2 Transition words will indicate order in time or space.

3 If there are not enough transition words, read the sentences to see what order they should be in according to their contents.

4 After putting statements in order, read them over to be sure the order is logical.

SELECTIONS FOR PRACTICE

SELECTION 1

A Then I'd love to go to the party and meet Pandora and her new boyfriend.

B First I'd like to go to that new Mexican restaurant that just opened and have some tacos.

1. Which is the correct order for these sentences?

   A A B

   B B A

SELECTION 2

A Next, you must mix the paint with the oil so that it has a smooth consistency.

B The first thing to do is make sure you buy the correct kind of paint so that it will not be too thin.

C Finally, you must place the mixture in a warm dry spot and let it sit for at least 24 hours before you use it.

2. Which is the correct order of these sentences?

   A A B C

   B B C A

   C B A C

   D A C B

SELECTION 3

A Two weeks after the class began, I was able to watch French movies without subtitles.

B After class I would go to a lab, where I would listen to special tapes that taught me vocabulary.

C Last year I joined a special intensive class that met every day for four and one-half hours.

D Now I can read French books with ease, and I can converse with almost no accent.

3.   Which is the correct order of these sentences?

   A   A B C D

   B   C B A D

   C   D B A C

   D   C A B D

SELECTION 4

A It's old and broken and not much use anyway.

B When I do, I'll throw away my typewriter.

C I can't wait to get my new computer.

4.   Which is the correct order of these sentences?

   A   C B A

   B   B C A

   C   B A C

   D   A C B

SELECTION 5

A Nor do I enjoy them stepping on my feet when they walk over me just to get a better waiting spot.

B I always hate going to train stations to wait for someone.

C They are so crowded and I don't like being jostled by a group of strangers.

5. Which is the correct order of these sentences?

    A   C B A

    B   B C A

    C   B A C

    D   C A B

SELECTION 6

A When we arrived, we were so exhausted that we went to bed before dinner.

B We went to visit the Barbours at their new home in Maine.

C After dinner the Barbours put on a spectacular magic show, which we unfortunately missed because we were still asleep.

6. Which is the correct order of these sentences?

    A   A B C

    B   B C A

    C   B A C

    D   C A B

14

WORD MEANINGS FROM CONTEXT

SAME MEANINGS

We can often derive the meaning of a new word from its **context**—that is, from the way it is used in a sentence or paragraph. For example, in the following paragraph, see if you can figure out which answer choice has the **same meaning** as the word *constraints*.

EXAMPLE 1

I had planned a visit to Egypt to see the pyramids, but financial constraints have made it impossible for me to pay for the trip. I hope my job situation improves soon, so I can spend money more freely.

1. *Constraints* means

   A duties.

   B music.

   C restrictions.

   D luck.

The correct answer is **C**, *restrictions*. When you substitute the word *restrictions* for *constraints*, you can see that the selection makes sense. None of the other answer choices does.

OPPOSITE MEANINGS

Sometimes you will be asked to read a word in context, determine its meaning, and then find a word **opposite** in meaning.

In the next example, find a meaning opposite to the meaning of *judiciously*.

EXAMPLE 2

I put all my earnings from my summer job into my bank account. If I spend my money judiciously, I should have enough to last me all year.

2. The OPPOSITE of *judiciously* is

   A wisely.

   B justly.

   C foolishly.

   D legally.

The correct answer is **C**, *foolishly*. We can determine from the context that the meaning of *judiciously* is "wisely." Therefore, the opposite is "foolishly."

MULTIPLE MEANINGS

Some words have multiple meanings. The meaning in a particular sentence or paragraph can be determined only by the context. For example, each of the three sentences below uses the word *present* in a different way.

EXAMPLE 3

1. He is the only member still present in the building.

2. The new car was the most expensive present he ever received.

3. He came to present a petition to the mayor on behalf of the union.

3. Which sentence uses the word *present* to mean "give"?

   A   1

   B   2

   C   3

The correct answer is **C**. The word give can be substituted for *present* in sentence 3, but not in sentences 1 or 2.

STRATEGIES AND TIPS
FOR FIGURING OUT MEANINGS FROM CONTEXT

1   Read the sentence that the unknown word is part of. If necessary, read the sentence before it and the sentence after it.

2   Guess what the word means. See if a word in the answer choices has the same meaning.

3   To check the answer choice, try using it in the original sentence.

4   If you need to pick an antonym, first decide on the word's meaning. Then a find a word among the answer choices that means the opposite.

5   When you need to choose between multiple meanings, try out the answer choices till you find one that fits the example.

SELECTIONS FOR PRACTICE

SELECTION 1

In an old fairy tale, when the prince drinks a potion, he turns into a frog. He stays a frog until a princess kisses him.

1. *Potion* means

    A   a low-calorie soda.

    B   a strange drink.

    C   a baby food.

    D   a strong soap.

SELECTION 2

By throwing all my papers in the filing cabinet and hiding all my junk behind the wall, I managed to give my office a semblance of order.

2. *Semblance* means

    A   financial savings.

    B   bad luck.

    C   appearance.

    D   maintenance.

SELECTION 3

There is obviously a strong affinity between Jack and Brenda. You could see it the moment they met. They got along so well. You'd think they were made for each other.

3. *Affinity* means

    A   dislike.

    B   boredom.

    C   skill.

    D   attraction.

SELECTION 4

When she wrote the first book, she thought there was nothing more to add to the story. But later she reconsidered and decided there was more to be told, so she wrote a sequel.

4. *Sequel* means

    A   continuation.

    B   savings.

    C   play.

    D   captive.

SELECTION 5

I've asked him twice whether or not he'd like to visit us, but he remains noncommittal. He won't give me a direct answer; he just says he'll let me know.

5. *Noncommittal* means

    A   angry or belligerent.

    B   giving no clear indication of a decision.

    C   tending toward sickness or feeling unwell.

    D   making a hasty decision.

SELECTION 6

He was a sweet-tempered baby, but as he got older he developed a pugnacious streak. Now he behaves as if he's always ready for a fight.

6. The opposite of *pugnacious* is

    A   content.

    B   self-assured.

    C   peaceful.

    D   shy.

SELECTION 7

The steamship captain said his yacht would ply the waters between Christie Island and Hadley until early January.

7. Which meaning of the word *ply* is used in this sentence?

    A   To use or practice

    B   To keep supplying

    C   To sail over regularly

    D   A thick layer, as in plywood

15

POETRY AND FIGURATIVE LANGUAGE

Poets, like other writers, sometimes tell a story in their poems, but often they want to communicate their experiences to us so that we may share them. These experiences might come from their observations of the world around them. Or they might come from their thoughts about life, death, and love.

In these first lines, the American poet Stephen Vincent Benét sets the stage for his poem about the American Civil War.

EXAMPLE 1

LEE

by Stephen Vincent Benét

The night had fallen on the narrow tent.
　　Deep night of Virginia summer when the stars
　　Are burning wax in the near, languid sky
And the soft flowers hardly close all night
But bathe in darkness, as a woman bathes
In a warm, fragrant water and distill
Their perfume still, without the fire of the sun.

1. What does this part of the poem describe?

   A　a narrow bed

   B　The fire of the sun

   C　A woman bathing in the dark

   D　A Virginia night in summer

Choice **D** is correct. The poet is describing a summer night in Virginia.

Read the next poem and decide how the poet feels about his land.

EXAMPLE 2

MY OWN LAND FOREVER

by John Greenleaf Whittier

Land of the forest and the rock,
Of dark blue lake and mighty river,
Of mountains reared on high to mock
The storm's career and lightning's shock,
My own green land forever!

2. The poet suggests that
   A   the land is untouched.
   B   the land will be cut up and developed.
   C   the land is highly populated.
   D   the land is all rocky.

Your teacher will discuss your answer.

What do we mean when we talk about the language of poetry? What makes a particular arrangement of words "feel like poetry"?

To answer these questions we must explore what it is that makes poetry different from other kinds of writing.

METER

Whenever we talk, we naturally stress certain words. Suppose you say:

She danced all night.

Notice how you stress the word *danced* and the word *night*. When you use a word of more than one syllable, you naturally stress one of the syllables. For example, if you say *wonderful*, you naturally stress the syllable *won*.

Rhythm is something you can tap your feet to. **Meter** is the name we give to the rhythm of poetry. It is the name used to describe a particular pattern of stressed sounds. They are also called **beats**.

Read the next example which comes from a poem by Edna St. Vincent Millay called "The Ballade of the Harp-Weaver." Notice which words or syllables you stress as you read the poem aloud.

EXAMPLE 3

> "Son," said my mother,
>
>   When I was knee-high,
>
> "You've need of clothes to cover you,
>
>   And not a rag have I.
>
> There's nothing in the house
>
>   To make a boy breeches,
>
> Nor shears to cut a cloth with
>
>   Nor thread to take stitches."

3. Where do the beats belong in this line? (Remember that the line over a word or syllable shows that it is stressed.)

    A   Nor shears to cut a cloth with

    B   Nor shears to cut a cloth with

    C   Nor shears to cut a cloth with

    D   Nor shears to cut a cloth with

Choice **C** is correct. The stress or beat is on the words *shears*, *cut*, and *cloth*.

NOTICE: Photocopying any part of this book is forbidden by law.

117

RHYME

Another technique that some poets use is to choose words that **rhyme**. The words that rhyme are usually the last words of the lines in a poem.

Read the verse by Whittier again. Notice the rhyming words.

> 1   **Land of the forest and the rock,**
>
> 2   **Of dark blue lake and mighty river,**
>
> 3   **Of mountains reared on high to mock**
>
> 4   **The storm's career and lightning's shock,**
>
> 5   **My own green land forever!**

In this poem, lines 1, 3, and 4 rhyme and lines 2 and 5 rhyme.

EXAMPLE 4

ONE PERFECT ROSE

by Dorothy Parker

1   **A single flow'r he sent me, since we met.**
      All tenderly his messenger he chose;
3   **Deep-hearted, pure, with scented dew still wet—**
      One perfect rose.

5   **I knew the language of the floweret;**
      "My fragile leaves," it said, "his heart enclose."
7   **Love long has taken for his amulet**
      One perfect rose.

9   **Why is it no one ever sent me yet**
      One perfect limousine, do you suppose?
11   **Ah no, it's always just my luck to get**
      One perfect rose.

    4A. The rhyme scheme is

      A   lines 1 and 2; 3 and 4.

      B   lines 1 and 3; 2 and 4.

      C   lines 1 and 4; 2 and 3.

      D   line 1, 2, and 3; 4 and 5.

4B. The poet seems to feel

   A   roses are too expensive.

   B   it would be nice to be sent a limousine instead of a rose.

   C   roses are expensive and don't last very long.

   D   she never gets roses.

 Your teacher will discuss your answers.

FREE VERSE

Not all poetry rhymes. Most modern poetry is written in **free verse**.

Free verse is called "free" because the poet is not required to follow set patterns of rhyme or of meter.

Read the next example and answer the question.

EXAMPLE 5

THE TWILIGHT

by Carmen Rivera

The morning light is dimming,
   Twilight is on its way,
   I am no longer the one you knew,
Or loved.
Grey locks combine with golden hair,
Lines etch the perfect face.
Time has come to stay at last,
Though, an unwanted guest.

5.   This poem is mostly about

   A   falling in love.

   B   aging.

   C   the morning light.

   D   golden hair.

This free verse poem is about aging. The poet speaks of grey hair, lines on her face, and the passage of time. The correct answer is **B**.

FIGURATIVE LANGUAGE

Writers often employ **figurative language** to express themselves in new and fresh ways. A writer may wish to say his sister was very scared. He might say, "her eyes revealed how frightened she was." Or he could use figurative language by saying, "Her eyes were like ghostly candles shining in the dark." This description tells us more vividly that she was very frightened.

Read the next poem by the American poet Emily Dickinson and decide on the meaning of the figurative language she uses.

EXAMPLE 6

THE CLOUDS

by Emily Dickinson

The clouds their backs together laid,
The north began to push,
The forest galloped till they fell,
The lightning skipped like mice . . .

How good to be safe in tombs,
Where nature's temper cannot reach,
Nor vengeance ever comes.

6.   The poet is describing

    A   death.

    B   a galloping horse.

    C   trees.

    D   mice.

Your teacher will discuss your answer.

SIMILES AND METAPHORS

When a comparison uses the words *like* or *as*, it is called a **simile**.

In Example 6, the poet used several similes to paint a picture of a storm.

The following example also contains a simile.

EXAMPLE 7

My old friend Tom is like a wild animal when he gets hungry. He eats all the food that isn't nailed down.

7.   In the simile in this passage, Tom is compared to

   A   something hungry.

   B   a wild animal.

   C   food.

   D   things that are nailed down.

Choice **B** is the correct answer. The author says that Tom is like a wild animal when he gets hungry. The word like tells you this is a simile.

When a comparison does not include the word *like* or *as*, it is called a **metaphor**. In Example 2, *twilight* serves as a metaphor for old age.

Find a metaphor in the following selection from the novel *To Kill a Mockingbird*, by Harper Lee.

EXAMPLE 8

Aunt Alexandra was fanatical on the subject of my attire. I could not possibly hope to be a lady if I wore breeches; when I said I could do nothing in a dress, she said I wasn't supposed to be doing things that required pants. Aunt Alexandra's vision of my deportment involved playing with small stoves, tea sets, and wearing the Add-A-Pearl necklace she gave me when I was born; furthermore, I should be a ray of sunshine in my father's lonely life. I suggested that one could be a ray of sunshine in pants just as well . . .

8A. In this selection, Scout, the narrator, is spoken of in a metaphor as someone who should be

    A   a ray of sunshine.

    B   doing nothing in a dress.

    C   playing with a tea set.

    D   an Add-a-Pearl necklace.

The correct choice is **A**. Aunt Alexandra says she "should be a ray of sunshine," which is a metaphor.

8B. What kind of things would Scout need to do to be the kind of "ray of sunshine" that her aunt would like her to be?

_____

_____

_____

_____

_____

 Your teacher will discuss your answer.

STRATEGIES AND TIPS
FOR UNDERSTANDING POETRY AND FIGURATIVE LANGUAGE

1   **Meter** refers to the way poets arrange the stressed sounds or beats into a pattern which is used in many or all the lines of a poem.

2   **Rhyme** refers to the technique used by many poets in which the last word of various lines rhyme.

3   Some poetry does not rhyme or have a meter. **Free verse** does not follow traditions such as rhyming or meter.

4   The term **figurative language** means using words and phrases in an unusual way where they don't mean exactly what they say.

5   Authors use figurative language to make their writing more colorful, powerful, and interesting. **Similes**, **metaphors**, and other kinds of figurative language help you see things in a new way.

6   You can usually use context clues to understand this language. Often, you need to read the whole passage or poem to understand words that are used figuratively.

SELECTIONS FOR PRACTICE

SELECTION 1

CLIMBING

by Amy Lowell

1 High up in the apple tree climbing I go,
  With the sky above me, the earth below.
3 Each branch is the step of a wonderful stair
  Which leads to the town I see shining up there.

5 Climbing, climbing, higher and higher,
  The branches blow and I see a spire,
7 The gleam of a turret, the glint of a dome,
  All sparkling and bright, like white sea foam.

  On and on, from bough to bough,
  The leaves are thick, but I push my way through;
  Before, I have always had to stop,
  But today I am sure I shall reach the top.

  Today to the end of the marvelous stair,
  Where those glittering pinnacles flash in the air!
  Climbing, climbing, higher I go,
  With the sky close above me, the earth far below.

1. The rhyme scheme for this poem is

 A lines 1 and 2; 3 and 4.

 B lines 1 and 3; 2 and 4.

 C lines 1 and 4; 2 and 3.

 D lines 1 and 5; 2 and 7.

SELECTION 2

VALENTINE

by Lewis Gardner

1 My love stirs in the breeze

2 Like paper hearts

3 Strung along the ceiling

4 Of the stationery store.

5 My love's a lacy heart

6 Packed with neat rows

7 Of extravagant treats.

8 Accept my heart—and bite

9 The crisp exterior

10 To reach the marshmallow

11 Beating inside.

2A. Lines 9, 10, and 11 mean the poet

  A is rich and powerful.

  B is young and strong.

  C is tough outside and soft inside.

  D is tired of people and wants to live in nature.

2B. Saying that "My love stirs in the breeze like paper hearts" is an example of

  A a simile.

  B a metaphor.

  C rhyme.

  D meter.

NOTICE: Photocopying any part of this book is forbidden by law.

125

SELECTION 3

A NIGHT WITH A WOLF

by Bayard Taylor

High up on the lonely mountains,
    Where the wild men watched and waited;
Wolves in the forest, and bears in the bush,
    And I on my path belated.

The rain and the night together
    Came down, and the wind came after,
Bending the props of the pine-tree roof,
    And snapping many a rafter.

I crept along in the darkness,
    Stunned, and bruised, and blinded;
Crept to a fir with thick-set boughs,
    And a sheltering rock behind it.

There, from the blowing and raining,
    Crouching, I sought to hide me.
Something rustled; two green eyes shone;
    And a wolf lay down beside me!

His wet fur pressed against me;
    Each of us warmed the other;
Each of us felt, in the stormy dark,
    That beast and man were brother.

And when the falling forest
    No longer crashed in warning,
Each of us went from our hiding place
    Forth in the wild, wet morning.

3A. Where do the beats belong in this line?

A   Wolves in the for-est, and bears in the bush

B   Wolves in the for-est, and bears in the bush

C   Wolves in the for-est, and bears in the bush

D   Wolves in the for-est, and bears in the bush

3B. What are the *roof* and *rafter* that are mentioned in the second stanza of the poem?

    A   the speaker's house

    B   tree branches in the forest

    C   a house that he tried to build

    D   a cottage in the forest

3C. The poet compares beast and man to

    A   a stormy night.

    B   brothers.

    C   a rock.

    D   green eyes.

3D. This poem is probably a fantasy, since wolves in nature are not likely to get close to people under any circumstances. If the man and wolf are metaphors for people who are usually enemies, what point might the poet be trying to make?

_____

_____

_____

_____

_____

_____

❖

16

EVERYDAY READING MATERIAL

Everyday reading selections include recipes, instructions, newspaper articles, advertisements, and letters. These materials can be studied with the same skills used for other kinds of selections. In addition, there are special features worth noting in some kinds of everyday reading material.

INSTRUCTIONS

Instructions tell you what to do. Because they also tell you the order in which to do something, instructions are often numbered or use key words that show order.

EXAMPLE 1

Instructions for Using Automatic Cash Machine.

1 Put credit card in slot.

2 Wait until screen turns yellow.

3 Type in amount of money desired.

4 Type in password.

5 Lift window and remove cash.

1.   According to these instructions, which sentence is correct?

A   Type in password before you put card in slot.

B   Type in cash desired before you put card in slot.

C   Type in cash desired before you type in password.

D   Type in password before you type cash desired.

The instructions tell you:

3 Type in amount of money desired.

4 Type in password.

Therefore, you type the password <u>after</u> you type the amount of cash desired. The correct choice is **C**.

Sometimes instructions are listed in a column but not numbered. The top instruction is done first, and so on, until we reach the bottom instruction, which is done last.

EXAMPLE 2

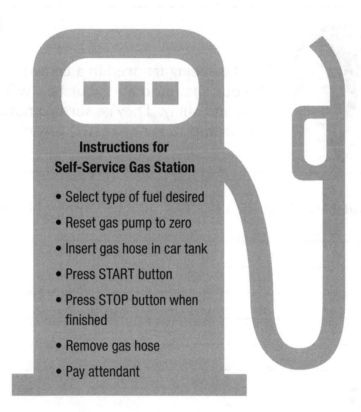

Instructions for Self-Service Gas Station

- Select type of fuel desired
- Reset gas pump to zero
- Insert gas hose in car tank
- Press START button
- Press STOP button when finished
- Remove gas hose
- Pay attendant

2. **Which statement is correct?**

A The gas pump is reset to zero immediately after pressing the STOP button.

B After inserting the gas hose in the tank, select the type of fuel desired.

C Remove the gas hose before you pay the attendant.

D Insert the hose in the tank immediately after you pay the attendant

The correct choice is **C**. *Pay attendant* is the last step, and *Remove gas hose* is done prior to making payment.

ADVERTISEMENTS

When we read advertisements, we need to look at the information that is included. We also need to analyze the persuasive language that is used. Advertisers cannot say things that are false. They might, however, suggest things that can't really be proven. And they will probably not include everything about their product—especially when the information will make the product seem less desirable.

EXAMPLE 3

Tired of being ignored in a crowd?
Use our shampoo and your hair will be
clean and shiny. They're sure to notice you.
Our shampoo is not tested on animals.

3. **Find a statement that is a fact, not an unprovable claim.**

_____

_____

_____

_____

_____

_____

Your teacher will discuss your answer.

EXAMPLE 4

There's no other hammer like the **Bang-O hammer**.

The best hammer you can buy, it features perfect balance, a comfortable handle, and a lifetime guarantee. Can be used at below-freezing temperatures and on all types of nails.

4. Which of these facts does NOT appear in the Bang-O ad?

   A   It is one of the most expensive hammers on the market.

   B   The handle is comfortable.

   C   It can be used in cold weather.

   D   It carries a lifetime guarantee.

Choice **A** is correct. An important fact not included in the ad is that the price is very high.

Sometimes ads are written in abbreviated form with words left out. For example, a proprietor may wish to state that his company buys and sells a variety of exercise machines, both those that run on electricity and mechanical ones. They may also buy and sell used machines and may run sales. An advertisement for this store may state this information in shortened form.

EXAMPLE 5

> ### EXERCISE MACHINES
>
> - New and used
> - Bought and sold
> - Electrical and mechanical
> - Frequent sales

5. This store is LEAST likely to

    A   sell new machines.

    B   offer machines at a low price.

    C   rent out machines for weekend use.

    D   buy used machines.

The correct answer is **C**. The store is least likely to rent out machines for weekends. The advertisement does not state that they provide this service. All the other alternatives are specifically stated in the ad.

LETTERS

There are two main kinds of letters:

- ❖ **friendly** letters, which provide a way to chat with friends, to extend messages of sympathy or thanks, or to invite people to events

- ❖ **business** letters, which are used to order products, deal with problems or legal requirements, and apply for jobs

Nowadays, some of our correspondence is done through e-mail or on the Internet, but people still must send letters in many circumstances.

EXAMPLE 6

Dear Fred,

I'm glad you can visit us over the weekend of the 24th. We'll expect you on Friday evening. The bus will drop you off at Main and Frost Streets. Use the phone on the corner and we'll pick you up. Try to get the 6 o'clock bus, which gets here at 7:15. Bring your skates because we play hockey on Saturday morning.

See you then,

Pete

6.   One detail Pete did NOT include in his letter is

   A   where Fred should get off the bus.

   B   the day he is expected.

   C   that he should bring his skates.

   D   the phone number Fred should call.

The letter does not include choice **D**, the phone number Fred should call. Fred, of course, may know the number already, but it could have been included in case he needed it with the other information.

STRATEGIES AND TIPS
FOR UNDERSTANDING EVERYDAY READING MATERIAL

1   The same techniques and skills are used with everyday reading materials as with other selections.

2   Look for key words or numerals when studying the sequence of recipes and other instructions.

3   Look closely at the details in everyday reading materials. Important information may have been left out.

4   Study the persuasive devices used in advertisements.

SELECTIONS FOR PRACTICE

SELECTION 1

1	Weigh clothes
2	Add correct amount of soap
3	Close top
4	Choose desired washing cycle
5	Pull out handle to start

1. These instructions are for

   A   a washing machine.

   B   a sewing machine.

   C   a dishwasher.

   D   an automatic car vacuum.

SELECTION 2

Gabrielle Mazzoni
476 Broadway
New York, NY 10013

Dear Traffic Bureau:

I received a parking ticket on June 3. My car was properly parked, although the ticket indicates I was near a fire hydrant. I would like to plead not guilty and would appreciate an appointment in the Night Traffic Court.

Sincerely,

Gabrielle Mazzoni

2. Which statement is NOT correct?

   A   Gabrielle was given a ticket.

   B   Gabrielle believes she is innocent.

   C   Gabrielle wants an appointment on June 3.

   D   Gabrielle wishes to plead not guilty.

SELECTION 3

Ms. Jones asked her secretary to buy a filing cabinet that had three drawers and a lock and that cost less than two hundred dollars. She also asked that the cabinet be in stock and available for delivery within 30 days or less. She said she preferred wood, but she would also accept steel or plastic. An advertisement for an office supplies store included several models.

3.   Which cabinet should the secretary buy?

   A   Model 100: 3 drawers, lock, $190, 90-day delivery, wood

   B   Model 180: 3 drawers, lock, $260, immediate delivery, wood

   C   Model 210: 3 drawers, lock, $230, 10-day delivery, wood

   D   Model 310: 3 drawers, lock, $190, 10-day delivery, steel

SELECTION 4

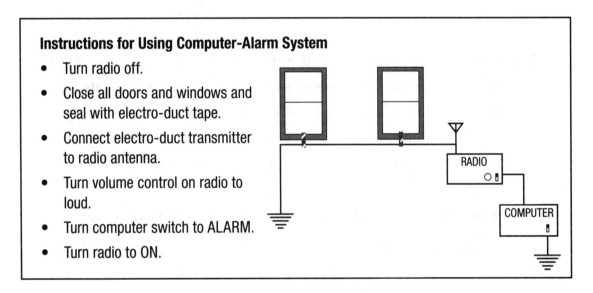

Instructions for Using Computer-Alarm System

- Turn radio off.
- Close all doors and windows and seal with electro-duct tape.
- Connect electro-duct transmitter to radio antenna.
- Turn volume control on radio to loud.
- Turn computer switch to ALARM.
- Turn radio to ON.

4.   The volume control on the radio is turned to loud

   A   after the computer switch is turned to ALARM.

   B   just before the radio is turned to OFF.

   C   after the transmitter is connected to the antenna.

   D   just after the radio is turned to ON.

SELECTION 5

Dear Rose,

The first few days of my vacation were about as unpleasant as any I've ever experienced. I signed up for this Desert Survival course in which we were going to learn to survive in the desert, without any special equipment, and without any help from anyone. At first we just worked hard, without ever talking to anyone in the class, or even to the teacher, and without any real sense of what we were going to do. By the end of the third day, I was disgusted. I almost quit.

However, it really worked out well. After about a week I got so I could handle almost any problem, and by the end of the second week, I had no trouble when I was left alone without food or water or any weapon. I can survive in the desert, and I'm confident I can handle any normal problem. Also, I made some really close friends, and found the whole vacation really worthwhile—although next year I'm just going to the beach and rest on the sand.

I hope to see you before school starts.

Lisa

5A. Which statement is NOT correct?

A   Lisa finished the course and developed survival skills.

B   Lisa decided survival skills were unimportant.

C   Lisa almost quit on the third day.

D   Lisa was silent on the first day of training.

5B. Write a letter from Rose to Lisa, responding to Lisa's letter.

_____

_____

_____

_____

_____

_____

SELECTION 6

Split Pea Soup

Put dried peas in water.

Bring water to boil.

Let sit one hour.

Drain and cover with water again.

Bring to boil and then simmer.

Add sliced carrots, ham bone, and garlic.

Cook two hours or until tender.

Serve with toasted French bread.

6. Which statement is correct?

   A   Bring to boil after you add carrots, ham, and garlic.

   B   Cook two hours and then add ham bone.

   C   Drain peas and let sit one hour.

   D   Cook two hours after adding carrots, ham, and garlic.

PART 3

PRACTICE TESTS

NOTICE: Photocopying any part of this book is forbidden by law.

139

PRACTICE TEST 1

This article describes an animal that seems to have a lot in common with human beings.

Some people feel a kinship with chimpanzees, the living creatures that most resemble humans in outward appearance. But scientists who have worked with dolphins often report that these creatures seem more like humans than any other animal.

Although dolphins look very different from us and live in the ocean in a manner far from our experience, they have much in common with the best of humans. Researchers have often stated that dolphins seem kinder, more intelligent, and more loving than most people. Many substantiated stories have described dolphins saving drowning humans, having fun with swimmers in the ocean, or playfully encircling small boats.

The dolphin is an awesome creature. It can swim underwater at about 35 miles an hour, can dive to great depths, and can navigate through underwater barriers with ease. Dolphins are powerful, able to kill a shark with apparent ease, yet playful and harmless to humans. Although hundreds of thousands of dolphins have been killed by human fisherman, there is no recorded incident of these beautiful animals ever having killed a human being.

Can we communicate with these intelligent sea-dwellers? Thus far, our success has been limited. Dolphins use a kind of underwater radar to navigate, and emit high-pitched whistles and clicks to communicate with each other. By using appropriate translation devices, Dr. John Lilly and his associates have attempted to carry on conversations with dolphins in English, and they report great success in this endeavor. Other scientists, however, have studied tape recordings of these conversations and remain unpersuaded that any communication actually took place. The issue is difficult to resolve, in part because some researchers have refused to do any work with captured dolphins. Studies are dependent upon captured dolphins, because hundreds of hours are required to teach them to communicate with us. Some of these studies have been terminated because researchers want dolphins to remain free. Dolphins are so like humans that some serious investigators want them to have the rights and freedoms enjoyed by humans.

1. According to the article, how do chimpanzees compare to dolphins?

   A   Dolphins look more like humans than chimpanzees do, and act more like humans.

   B   Chimpanzees resemble humans more in their outer appearance, but dolphins have more human characteristics.

   C   Dolphins resemble humans more in their outer appearance, but chimpanzees have more human characteristics.

   D   Neither chimpanzees nor dolphins are as kind and loving as the majority of human beings.

2. The author probably feels that

   A   research with dolphins is silly.

   B   research with dolphins could prove valuable.

   C   dolphins are very unintelligent.

   D   chimpanzees are more important than dolphins.

3. Which statement contains an opinion?

   A   Dolphins can kill sharks.

   B   Dolphins make high-pitched sounds under water.

   C   Dolphins have more human traits than chimpanzees.

   D   Dolphins can swim as fast as 35 miles per hour.

4. Which of these reasons is most important in making scientists feel that dolphins are intelligent?

    A   They are very beautiful.

    B   They can kill sharks.

    C   They can swim at speeds approaching 35 m.p.h.

    D   They communicate with each other.

5. According to this selection, why do some investigators refuse to conduct research on the dolphin?

    A   Investigators want the dolphin to be free.

    B   Investigators find the dolphin impossible to train.

    C   Investigators don't want to harm dolphins in their nets.

    D   None of the above.

6. According to this article, it is a fact that Dr. Lilly has

    A   tried to converse with dolphins.

    B   succeeded in conversing with dolphins.

    C   wanted to free captive dolphins.

    D   taught English to dolphins.

7. Compare dolphin behavior to human behavior. Describe how the behavior of the two species is similar and how it is different. Use details from the article to support your answer.

    _____

    _____

    _____

    _____

    _____

    _____

♣

The speaker of this poem is thinking about one of the tunnels under the Hudson River through which cars, trucks, and buses drive to New York City.

UNDER THE HUDSON

by Lev Sadovnik

When you drive a tunnel approach,
You never face the water;
The engineers aim you toward land.

If you saw the glistening waves,
The seagulls, the barges,
A hole that leads under water—

Would you dare?
Which of our journeys would we begin
If the route were clearly marked?

8. The first line of this poem is:

    "When you drive a tunnel approach,"

    How could this line be restated?

    A   When you drive your car into a tunnel

    B   When you take a picture of a tunnel

    C   When you try to get clean air in a tunnel

    D   When you choose stones to build a tunnel

9. The first three lines of this poem suggest that engineers of tunnels

    A   are confused about how to build tunnels.

    B   try to get you to drive longer distances.

    C   prefer digging tunnels under land.

    D   don't want drivers to see that they are about to drive under water.

10. "Glistening waves," "seagulls," and "barges" are details to help a reader picture

    A   the apprehension caused by driving into water.

    B   things seen when going toward the tunnel.

    C   an underwater tunnel.

    D   typical problems for a tunnel engineer.

11. The poem suggests a similarity between

    A   life's journeys and driving into a tunnel.

    B   bad signs on a highway and life in New York City.

    C   the need for clear road signs and problems with building tunnels.

    D   seagulls and road signs.

12. The author writes,

> "Which of our journeys would we begin
> If the route were clearly marked?"

What do these lines suggest about the poet's viewpoint of life? Use details from the poem in your answer.

_____

_____

_____

_____

_____

_____

❖

People in his own time weren't sure of Sam Houston's place in history. Read this article about him and judge for yourself.

Sam Houston was one of the most colorful figures in American history. A daring soldier and statesman, he became a legend in his own time. Houston played a key role in shaping the history of Texas from the time it was a Mexican territory to the time of the American Civil War.

Born in 1793, Houston grew up in Virginia. When he was still a boy, he ran away from home to live with the Cherokee Indians. This experience was to influence him for the rest of his life.

In 1813, Houston joined the American army, a year after the War of 1812 broke out between the United States and England. After the war he worked for the U. S. Government's Indian Bureau, trying to win rights for the Cherokees. However, Houston could not stay in one place for long. He resigned from the Indian Bureau and moved to Tennessee. There he practiced law until he entered politics. Houston served in the U.S. House of Representatives (1823-1827) and as governor of Tennessee (1827-1829). Then he abruptly resigned as governor and went to live once more with his beloved Cherokees. He married a Cherokee woman, Tiana Rogers, in 1830.

Three years later, Houston was seized with the urge to move on. He rode into Texas, then a part of Mexico, where he became a leader among the American settlers. In 1836, Texas signed its Declaration of Independence from Mexico, and Houston was made commander-in-chief of the Texas army. He went on to win a decisive victory against larger forces. With fewer than 1,000 men, General Houston beat back an army of 6,000 at the Battle of San Jacinto. Overnight, Texas became an independent republic and Houston was a hero.

Houston served twice as president of the Lone Star Republic of Texas. After Texas was admitted to the Union, Houston served as one of the state's senators (1846-1859). During most of these years, he was still a hero in the eyes of the Texans. However, he made some enemies while he was senator by becoming the only Southerner to oppose slavery. Starting in 1859, when Houston was elected governor of Texas, his political career began to go downhill. His continuing concern for the fate of Native Americans was unpopular, and a real break came when he opposed the people's wish to break away from the Union and join the Confederacy of Southern states. On this issue he was forced out of office in 1863. He died in the same year. Often misunderstood in his lifetime, Houston became, to later generations, a symbol of strength, independence, and the pioneer spirit.

13. According to this article, Sam Houston is mainly remembered for his role in

    A   the War of 1812.

    B   the history of Texas.

    C   the politics of Tennessee.

    D   the Civil War.

14. Here are some of the events of Sam Houston's life:

    Which part of Houston's career belongs in the empty box?

    A   lived with Cherokees

    B   opposed secession of Texas

    C   senator from Texas

    D   served in U. S. House of Representatives

15. Which of the following statements is an opinion, NOT a fact?

    A   Houston was a symbol of strength and independence.

    B   Houston was commander-in-chief of the Texas army.

    C   Houston resigned from the Indian Bureau.

    D   Houston was a leader among the American settlers in Texas.

16. According to the article, a major factor in Houston's life was

    A   difficulty in taking responsibility.

    B   being unpopular with people.

    C   hatred for Native Americans.

    D   a desire to move to new places.

17. Which of these was NOT a reason that Houston's experience at San Jacinto made people consider him a hero?

    A   His army won.

    B   He fought against a much larger army.

    C   It established the independence of Texas.

    D   It was the first battle in which he had ever participated.

18. Texans showed their positive regard for Houston by

    A   forcing him out of office.

    B   electing him president and senator.

    C   signing a declaration of independence.

    D   opposing slavery.

19. According to the article, Houston was the only Southern senator to oppose

    A   independence for Texas.

    B   rights for Native Americans.

    C   slavery.

    D   the Bureau of Indian Affairs.

20. Houston was forced out of office as governor of Texas because he opposed

    A   the Union.

    B   the fate of Native Americans.

    C   any military action.

    D   joining the Confederacy.

21. The author says that many people considered Sam Houston to be "a symbol of strength, independence, and the pioneer spirit." What details does he use in this article to support this opinion of Sam Houston?

_____

_____

_____

_____

_____

_____

NOTICE: Photocopying any part of this book is forbidden by law.

147

Ricardo read about a job available after school at the mall. He wrote this letter in order to apply for it.

784 Main Street
Highland Park, IL 60035
Sept. 18, 2000

Manager
Everykid Toy Store
Westside Mall
Highland Park, IL 60035

Dear Manager:

I would like to apply for the sales clerk job that you advertised in this week's *Town Gazette*. I am available to begin work after October 1.

I am 16 years old and a sophomore at Abraham Lincoln High School. I have been on the swim team for three years and I have earned my lifesaving certificate.

Although I have never worked in a store, I was one of the crew chiefs for the Boy Scout toy drive for two years, and I have helped my aunt and uncle organize their antiques and collectibles for the Highland Park Flea Market every week since I was eleven. I am a very enthusiastic and hard worker.

My references are my social studies teacher, Ms. Jamal, and my swimming coach, Mr. LoPresti. They will answer any questions about me if you call them at Abraham Lincoln High School, 555-6240.

I will be happy to come to the store for an interview. Please phone me at 555-8592.

Sincerely yours,

Ricardo Suarez

22. Ricardo's purpose in writing this letter is to

   A   explain why swimming is good experience.

   B   convince the manager to interview him.

   C   explain why he needs a job.

   D   suggest that selling toys is hard work.

23. Ricardo mentioned the toy drive and helping his aunt and uncle because

    A   the manager is a friend of his uncle's.

    B   he thinks his experience could be applied to the job at the store.

    C   everyone likes the Boy Scouts.

    D   they show he is a generous person.

24. Ricardo does NOT mention in his letter

    A   having worked as a lifeguard.

    B   going to school.

    C   practical experience.

    D   having people who will serve as references.

25. Which is an opinion?

    A   I have never worked in a store.

    B   I have earned my lifesaving certificate.

    C   I am 16 years old and a sophomore at Abraham Lincoln High School.

    D   I am a very enthusiastic and hard worker.

26. Ricardo probably mentioned the swim team and lifesaving certificate to

    A   get a job as a lifeguard.

    B   show that he is dependable.

    C   prepare for working in the swimming pool department of the store.

    D   show that he can swim.

We don't often think much about the sense of smell. According to the following article, people who lose it realize how important it is.

Most people take their ability to smell for granted. But there are some people who cannot smell a thing. Even if you cook supper right next to them or burn the toast, they won't smell anything.

Two million Americans suffer from anosmia, the inability to smell. They can distinguish flowers by appearance, but the smell of a rose or a lilac is lost to them. Amazingly, some have brief periods of time, perhaps a few hours a year, when the sense of smell returns. Every such moment can seem a miracle but then, incomprehensibly, the door slams shut again and the sense of smell has gone. People who have lost this sense are at risk in all sorts of ways. They can't smell fire or spoiled food or gas leaks.

There is no medical treatment for anosmia.

At the opposite end of the spectrum are the connoisseurs of smell, the geniuses of the nose. Helen Keller was one; she could perform prodigies of perception by odor alone. Since she was both blind and deaf, the sense of smell was very important to her; she developed it into an instrument of sensitivity and depth. She once wrote:

> The sense of smell has told me of a coming storm hours before there was any sign of it visible. I notice first a throb of expectancy, a slight quiver, a concentration in my nostrils. As the storm draws near my nostrils dilate, the better to receive the flood of earth odors which seem to multiply and extend, until I feel the splash of rain against my cheek. As the tempest departs, receding farther and farther, the odors fade, become fainter and fainter, and die away beyond the bar of space.

If Helen Keller were alive today, she might be offered a job by one of the companies making perfumes. Many of their employees are professors of odors, able to tell thousands of ingredients by subtle differences in smell, to blend the tiniest quantities into a new perfume, and to pick out the faintest difference between similar perfumes.

27. The author seems surprised that

    A   some people with anosmia can smell odors a few hours each year.

    B   there is no medical treatment for anosmia.

    C   two million people suffer from anosmia.

    D   people with anosmia can't smell spoiled food.

28. The expression *the door slams shut again* means that people with anosmia

    A   forgot they were once ill.

    B   go back to their families.

    C   lose the sense of smell again.

    D   suddenly feel happy.

29. The author seems to feel that the sense of smell

    A   is unimportant for people who can see.

    B   is important for a few hours each year.

    C   can make life fuller and happier.

    D   can be improved by drugs and medical treatment.

30. This web shows details about the condition known as "anosmia." What detail belongs in the empty circle?

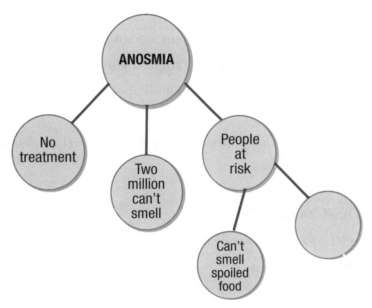

A   can't smell roses

B   smell returns for short time

C   can't smell fire

D   help create perfumes

31. You can infer from Helen Keller's words that the odors of the earth were strongest

A   about half an hour before the storm.

B   minutes before the storm.

C   about a half-hour after the storm.

D   the evening after the storm ends.

32. According to this article, what are some of the ways that a sense of smell is important to people?

_____

_____

_____

_____

_____

_____

❖

In this story, the Germans have just won a war against France and are taking over a part of the country. François is a French boy who is studying great French literature. The whole class is conducted in French.

THE LAST LESSON

by Alphonse Daudet

I started out a little late so I had to rush to get to school. Also I didn't know the lesson and I was afraid Mr. Hamel would shout at me. I didn't want to go to school. It was so warm and light. The birds were singing in the woods. The German soldiers were marching up and down. I wanted to stay away from school. But I was strong enough to resist and I hurried to my class.

I passed the town hall on the way to school. People were reading the bulletin board. For the last two years all the news was bad. The bulletin board had all the news from our army. It told of the battles we lost. It told that Germany beat us in the war. It told what new rules we had to follow.

When I got to school it was quiet. Usually it was noisy when we first got there. Desks and drawers and closets were opening. Kids were talking and practicing lessons. Usually I could sneak to my desk without being seen because of the noise and confusion.

When I walked in late I was very scared. But today Mr. Hamel didn't punish me. He said in a kind way, "Go to your desk, little François. We are beginning."

Mr. Hamel was dressed in his beautiful green coat. He wore his fine shirt and his black silk cap, which was only for special days. The benches in back were usually empty, but today they were filled with people. The former mayor, Mr. Hausen, sat there with his three-cornered hat. So did a lot of other important people.

I wondered what was happening. Then Mr. Hamel spoke. "Boys and girls, this is your last lesson. We have received new orders. Now the school will teach only in German. Today I teach you your last lesson in French. Tomorrow a new teacher will be here. Pay attention."

Now I knew what the people were reading on the bulletin board. How horrible I felt. This was my last lesson in French and I hardly had learned anything. I wished I had gone to school more and learned more. I used to think my books were too heavy and I wished they were gone. But now I thought they were old friends. I didn't want to give them up. I was even sorry I couldn't see Mr. Hamel again although he was always shouting.

Then Mr. Hamel called my name. He asked me a question which I couldn't answer. I got mixed up and just stood there, holding onto my desk. My heart was beating fast and I didn't dare to look up.

Mr. Hamel said, "I won't scold you, François. You must feel bad enough. Every day we say, 'I'll learn it tomorrow. There's no rush.' But now you see what happens. And you're not the worst, François. We're all to blame. Your parents let you stay home to help with the farm. I sent you to water my flowers. We are all to blame."

"You must never forget your language. French is beautiful. As long as you keep your language you will never be a slave."

Then he gave us a lesson. Everyone was quiet and worked hard.

33. Why was François scared when he entered his classroom?

    A   Mr. Hamel was dressed in a green coat.

    B   François was late.

    C   François forgot his books.

    D   The mayor was there.

34. François said that he knew what people were reading on the bulletin board. What do you think they were reading?

    A   a notice about staying out late

    B   a notice saying that German would be taught in schools

    C   a notice about working longer hours and getting less pay

    D   a notice saying that schools would be closed

35. François says that the benches in the back of the room are usually empty. Why are they full now?

  A   Mr. Hamel is teaching the last lesson in French.

  B   The former mayor is taking over the class.

  C   The new teacher is being introduced.

  D   It is a day of celebration.

36. In the future, François will probably

  A   enroll in another school.

  B   be better at German than French.

  C   learn to speak German.

  D   want to learn Italian.

37. How does François's attitude about his studies change by the end of the story?

  A   He thinks studying is very foolish.

  B   He is sorry he didn't study more.

  C   He feels he will learn more in German.

  D   He dislikes his books.

38. What theme does this story teach? Use details from the passage to support your answer.

_____

_____

_____

_____

_____

_____

PRACTICE TEST 2

According to this article, animals may make music for some of the reasons people do.

Early people painted wonderful colored pictures. We still have some of these preserved on cave walls. Probably these cave dwellers also beat out rhythms by pounding bones one against another, beating on hollow trees, singing and shouting around the fire. But unlike the cave paintings bequeathed to us by the people who lived long ago, we have no way of proving that music is just as old as painting.

Yet scientists like Lewis Thomas argue that music is so endemic throughout the animal world that early people must have made music, also. Professor Thomas gives many examples of animals that make sounds, not just to communicate, but for pleasure. He states that the pleasure of hearing sounds is built into almost all animal life. We are creatures who love music.

Bird songs are the most obvious example of music among animals. Some bird song has a practical purpose. Birds sing to seek a mate, to make alarm calls, and to assert their claim to their territory. But most bird song has no purpose that we know about; probably its only function is for pleasure. The nightingale's enormous repertoire of variations on 24 basic songs isn't intended for specific messages. Most of the time, the nightingale seems to be singing just to enjoy its own songs.

Animals make sounds any way they can. Woodpeckers pound their heads against trees, gorillas beat their chests, rattlesnakes rattle their tails, fish blow air. A tiny one-inch beetle, *Lepinotus inquilinus*, makes a soft sound we can just barely hear; the hawk moth makes easily audible high-pitched sounds like a clarinet; termites call and respond to one another by beating their heads against the ground. Some of these sounds are made to communicate within the species. Some are used in work. Some are probably just to have a good time.

Bats provide a good example of the different way animals use sound. Bats send out high-pitched sounds so effectively that they can locate a tiny insect in the dark. These are the sounds they make when they are at work, but when they rest, head down, after a long night of hunting, they make beautiful bell-like tones that resemble music.

Some of the sounds animals make are for pleasure. We can assume that, as with humans, music brings joy. We can also be nearly certain that early people beat out rhythms and made music to make themselves happy.

1. We can't be sure early people made music because

   A   music can't be made in caves.

   B   people were too busy painting pictures.

   C   music didn't leave any traces.

   D   hunters cannot make music because it alerts their prey.

2. In the phrase "unlike the records bequeathed to us by early painters," the word *bequeathed* means

   A   destroyed.

   B   left behind.

   C   drawn or painted.

   D   made by fire.

3. What detail belongs in the empty space?

Animals	Sounds
Gorillas	Beat chest
Beetle	Makes tiny sound
Termites	
Hawk moth	Sounds like a clarinet
Bats	High-pitched sound
Fish	Blow air

   A   Beautiful bell-like tones

   B   Rattle tails

   C   Music

   D   Beating heads on ground

4. When the author writes that "music is so endemic throughout the animal world," the word *endemic* means

   A   harmful.

   B   found everywhere.

   C   healing.

   D   dangerous.

5. The author of this passage would probably agree that

   A   the love of music is inborn and not the result of training.

   B   animals make sounds primarily as a warning to other animals.

   C   early humans preferred painting to music.

   D   modern-day television will turn people away from an interest in music.

6. The author says the nightingale has an enormous *repertoire* of songs. Who else would have an enormous repertoire in his or her trade?

   A   a clown with a small red nose

   B   a comedian who knows 1,000 jokes

   C   a very fast runner

   D   a woman who owns a beautiful old violin

7. Look at the ways musical sounds are made in the animal kingdom. Compare some of these with the ways that people make music. Use several examples from the article in your answer.

   _____

   _____

   _____

   _____

   _____

   _____

❖

Romeo has fallen in love with Juliet. His family is the Montagues, bitter enemies of Juliet's family, the Capulets. Right after meeting her, Romeo has just climbed the wall around her house.

Juliet
Art thou not Romeo, and a Montague?

Romeo
Neither, fair maid, if either thee dislike.

Juliet
How camest thou hither, tell me, and wherefore?
The orchard walls are high and hard to climb,
And the place death, considering who thou art,
If any of my kinsmen find thee here.

Romeo
With love's light wings did I o'erperch these walls;
For stony limits cannot hold love out,
And what love can do, that dares love attempt.
Therefore thy kinsmen are no stop to me.

Juliet
If they do see thee, they will murder thee.

Romeo
Alack, there lies more peril in thine eye
Than twenty of their swords! Look thou but sweet,
And I am proof against their enmity.

Juliet
I would not for the world they saw thee here.

Romeo
I have night's cloak to hide me from their eyes;
And but thou love me, let them find me here.

8. When Juliet asks Romeo why he came to her home, she says it is "death, considering who thou art." What does Juliet mean?

    A There are deadly plants in the orchard.

    B Juliet's family would kill Romeo for being there.

    C Montagues tend to die young.

    D She wants him to take dangerous risks.

9. What are "love's light wings" that Romeo says helped him "o'erperch these walls"?

    A   a small aircraft

    B   a ladder

    C   the strength he has because he is in love

    D   two feathered devices that he strapped to his shoulders

10. What is the *enmity* that Romeo faces?

    A   a serious disease

    B   a change for the worse in the weather

    C   the possibility that Juliet doesn't love him

    D   Juliet's relatives' hatred

11. When Romeo says, "I have night's cloak to hide me from their eyes," he means

    A   the darkness will protect him.

    B   he has a dark coat on.

    C   he is invisible.

    D   he is hiding in the hall.

12. What problem do Romeo and Juliet face? What is Romeo's attitude about it? Use details from the play to support your answer.

    _____

    _____

    _____

    _____

    _____

    _____

❖

Spicy Mushroom and Sausage Pasta

Chop 2 onions, 1 pound mushrooms, and 3 cloves garlic.

Microwave 4 spicy sausage for 2 minutes and cool.

Slice sausage and fry together with mushrooms, garlic, and onions in 3 tablespoons of olive oil.

Add cooked pasta and taste for seasoning.

Serve with grated cheese.

13. This information comes from
   - **A**   a book of funny stories.
   - **B**   a book on how to make cheese.
   - **C**   a manual on how to use a stove.
   - **D**   a cookbook.

14. After cooking the sausage, which step comes next?
   - **A**   Add the cooked pasta.
   - **B**   Chop the mushrooms.
   - **C**   Cook the pasta.
   - **D**   Slice the sausage.

15. Which ingredient is NOT used in this recipe?
   - **A**   onion
   - **B**   garlic
   - **C**   salt
   - **D**   olive oil

This poem is written by Lewis Carroll, a famous English writer, and appears in his book **Through the Looking Glass.**

THE WALRUS AND THE CARPENTER

by Lewis Carroll

The sun was shining on the sea,
Shining with all his might;
He did his very best to make
The billows smooth and bright—
And this was odd, because it was
The middle of the night.

The Walrus and the Carpenter
were walking close at hand;
They wept like anything to see
Such quantities of sand;
"If this were only cleared away,"
They said, "it would be grand!"
"If seven maids with seven mops
Swept it for half a year,
Do you suppose," the Walrus said,
"That they could get it clear?"
"I doubt it," said the Carpenter,
And shed a bitter tear.

"O Oysters, come and walk with us!"
The Walrus did beseech.
"A pleasant walk, a pleasant talk,
Along the briny beach;
We cannot do with more than four,
To give a hand to each."

The eldest Oyster looked at him,
But never a word he said;
The eldest Oyster winked his eye,
And shook his heavy head—
Meaning to say he did not choose
to leave the oyster bed.

But four young Oysters hurried up,
All eager for the treat;
Their coats were brushed, their faces washed,
Their shoes were clean and neat—
And this was odd, because, you know,
They hadn't any feet.

The Walrus and the Carpenter
Walked on a mile or so,
And then they rested on a rock
Conveniently low;
And all the little Oysters stood
And waited in a row.

"The time has come," the Walrus said,
"To talk of many things:
Of shoes—and ships—and sealing wax,
Of cabbages and kings—
And why the sea is boiling hot—
And whether pigs have wings.
A loaf of bread," the Walrus said,
"Is what we chiefly need;
Pepper and vinegar besides
Are very good indeed—
Now if you're ready, Oysters dear,
We can begin to feed."

"But not on us!" the Oysters cried,
Turning a little blue.
"After such kindness, that would be
A dismal thing to do!"
"The night is fine!" the Walrus said,
"Do you admire the view?"

"I weep for you," the Walrus said,
"I deeply sympathize."
With sobs and tears he sorted out
Those of the largest size,
Holding his pocket handkerchief
Before his streaming eyes.

"O Oysters," said the Carpenter,
"You've had a pleasant run!
Shall we be trotting home again?"
But answer came there none—
And this was scarcely odd, because
They'd eaten every one.

16. What was odd about the fact that the sun was shining?

    A   It was cloudy.

    B   It was the middle of the night.

    C   It was raining.

    D   It was winter.

17. Which character in the poem turned down the Walrus's invitation to walk along the beach?

    A   the Carpenter

    B   the eldest Oyster

    C   the cabbages

    D   the four little Oysters

18. What was odd about the fact that the little Oysters were wearing shoes?

    A   The little Oysters had put their shoes on backwards.

    B   The little Oysters hadn't tied their shoelaces.

    C   The little Oysters didn't have any feet.

    D   The little Oysters wore only socks.

19. After they sat down, the Walrus proposed

    A   a long discussion on many strange subjects.

    B   a brief nap in the shade.

    C   a refreshing dip in the ocean.

    D   a trip to the market.

20. Which proposal did the Walrus make next?

   A   sending the little Oysters home

   B   walking to the nearest restaurant

   C   having a meal on the spot

   D   swimming in the ocean

21. Why did the Oysters turn "a little blue"?

   A   They were feeling cold after their walk.

   B   They were afraid they were going to be eaten.

   C   They were faint from hunger.

   D   They were putting makeup on.

22. Which of the following is true?

   A   The Walrus felt so sorry for the Oysters that he let them go free.

   B   The Walrus was mopping his eyes with his handkerchief and did not see the Oysters escape.

   C   The Walrus pretended to sympathize with the Oysters' fate while he selected the largest ones for a meal.

   D   The Walrus didn't have much of an appetite.

23. What details in the poem support the opinion that this poem is intended to amuse its audience?

_____

_____

_____

_____

_____

_____

Some people can't sing well. They have very poor ears. No one knows why they can't hear when they sing off key. Scientists don't even know what causes it.

When Abraham Mayhew was nine, his teacher picked him for a part in the school play, which was half a musical show and half a serious drama. Abe Mayhew played the part of a pirate who sailed the seas near the coast of Africa, preying on British and American merchant vessels, attacking the ships and stealing their cargo. Although Abe was the smallest boy in the class and was usually very shy and quiet, he was a wonderful actor and became a fierce and terrifying personage on stage.

There was only one problem. He was supposed to sing two lines on stage and he was unable to get them right. No matter how much he practiced, he couldn't seem to sing on key. Finally, his teacher told him to just say the words.

Abe's mother and father were both musicians and both of his brothers and his sister played instruments. They all could learn to sing Abe's lines in just one minute. All of them, especially his five-year-old brother, tried to help Abe practice, but finally everyone gave up.

A small number of people cannot learn to sing on key. They are more or less tone-deaf, or musically impaired. Like Abe Mayhew, they are perfectly normal people with perfectly normal hearing—except for music. They are kings and scientists and athletes and mothers and generals, often distinguished members of society. They could be trusted to lead big companies or armies or to lead their nation in peacetime or in war, but they couldn't be trusted to sing one minute's worth of "Happy Birthday to You."

Singing on key, or "pitch discrimination" as scientists call it, is a mysterious talent. Some people, erroneously thought to be tone-deaf, have made marvelous progress with the help of musically trained teachers. Others are in the same situation as Abraham Mayhew, unable to make much progress despite painstaking effort.

Scientists who have studied musical talent have made very little progress. They seem to have traveled only a few feet on the long road to understanding why and how we listen to music. Spoken and written language seem to be encoded in the left part of the brain. Music, as well as artistic skills, are in the right brain. That's about all we know so far. In the next fifty years we'll know a lot more than that about the parts of the brain that underlie musical talent.

Music puzzles scientists because it doesn't seem to have any survival value. We can understand that learning and seeing and tasting and feeling help us to survive. But why is the love of music important? If Abraham Mayhew lost his vision or feeling or hearing or taste sensations, he would need a lot of help to survive. But he can live very well without the ability to hear the difference in pitch from one song to another.

Abe says that one way or another, he can tell when they play "The Star Spangled Banner," so he knows it's time to stand up. He wishes he could do more than that. His friends and his family love music. He wishes he could enjoy it as they do.

24. Abraham Mayhew's kid brother

   A   sang worse than Abe.

   B   sang about as well as Abe.

   C   sang much better than Abe.

   D   hated music.

25. The author seems to think that Abe will

   A   lose his hearing completely.

   B   never learn to sing on key.

   C   sing on key but never play an instrument.

   D   eventually be a fine musician.

26. The author says that scientists *have traveled a few feet on the long road to understanding* music. This means scientists have

   A   made no progress in understanding music.

   B   completely understood how we learn music.

   C   made a lot of progress in understanding music.

   D   made a little progress in understanding music.

27. Taste has "survival value" because it helps us

    A   enjoy sweet food like ice cream.

    B   avoid spoiled food which would make us sick.

    C   keep our teeth clean and free of cavities.

    D   know where to find water.

28. A person with poor "pitch discrimination"

    A   doesn't sing well.

    B   is intelligent.

    C   is not likely to live long.

    D   will lose all of his or her friends.

29. Which fact is most important in this selection?

    A   Abe's teacher told him not to sing on stage.

    B   Abe's father and mother were musicians.

    C   Abe couldn't learn to sing on key.

    D   Abe is shy but he's a wonderful actor.

30. Which statement is an opinion?

    A   Abe's teacher told him not to sing on stage.

    B   Abe was the smallest boy in the class.

    C   Both of Abe's brothers play a musical instrument.

    D   Abe was a wonderful actor.

31. Is the ability to hear music important for most people? Why or why not? Use details from the article in your answer.

_____

_____

_____

_____

_____

_____

In the following story, a boy makes his own paradise.

PARADISE

by Maribel Ruiz

Dwayne's interest in trees and the environment happened quite accidentally. Of course, he was aware of the environmental issues that filled the newspapers, but Dwayne's interest was more specific. He was interested in the small portion of environment that was his backyard. On a shopping trip one afternoon, he noticed several tropical trees for sale in front of a large discount store. The trees looked like what one might see on a tropical island or rain forest. They certainly didn't look like they belonged in a big modern city.

Dwayne looked to see how much one of the trees cost. It was a little more than twelve dollars, which was about how much Dwayne had in his pocket. On an impulse, he bought one. It looked lonely in his yard so as soon as he had some more money he got a second. The second one was covered with brilliantly colored flowers. Soon he was buying more and more trees and plants, and his yard was fast becoming transformed into a tropical paradise.

Winter was approaching. Dwayne knew his tropical rain forest wouldn't survive when the air chilled. He couldn't move the trees into his house. Then Dwayne had an idea. He rigged up a shelter consisting of large wooden poles covered with transparent plastic, which prevented warm air from escaping. When it got too cold, he kept the tent warm by heating it. He kept some water inside his tent to make the climate of the tent humid, and then he was set.

One night Dwayne went into his little backyard forest. He could see the stars twinkling through the plastic. He could smell the flowering

trees. He lay down on a cot he had brought outside and looked up at the sky, letting the sweet, moist air envelop him.

Dwayne thought he could hear birds. He looked up and there were toucans and parrots in the trees overhead. The brightly colored tropical birds resembled the flowers that covered the trees. And the trees seemed to have grown. He thought he saw something else moving through them. Looking closely, he could see monkeys swinging through the branches. His forest was alive. He got up and walked around. The rain forest seemed much larger than his yard. He thought he saw a green vine coiled around a tree, until the vine moved and he realized it was a snake. Dwayne didn't understand what was happening in his little backyard, but it suited him perfectly.

Every time Dwayne went into his yard he noticed more. He saw trees he didn't remember planting. Butterflies danced around him. Insects larger than he had ever seen scurried over the ground. Dwayne decided to explore his rain forest. He began walking, expecting to quickly reach the edge of the plastic tent. But instead, he kept walking further and further into a forest. After a while he came to a little stream. Following the stream, he came across a tall waterfall that fell into a pool. Dwayne couldn't resist. He dived into the pool and played there, spinning around and then going deep underwater. It was a wonderful playground.

Suddenly Dwayne heard something splash next to him. A second later, a boy of about his own age came out of the water. After Dwayne overcame his surprise, he said hello to the boy. There was no answer. Dwayne tried again. The boy said something to Dwayne, but Dwayne didn't understand him. The boy obviously didn't speak English, and Dwayne didn't understand a word he said, either.

But the boys understood the language of play and companionship. With time, they learned a smattering of each other's language as well. Every afternoon after school, Dwayne rushed to his rain forest, looking forward to seeing his friend. The boy, Andoo, knew the ways of the forest well. He taught Dwayne how to climb the trees and gather the fruit. He taught him how to fish and hunt. They played under the waterfall, swimming and diving in the pool.

Months and then years passed. Sometimes Andoo asked Dwayne about the world outside the rain forest. Dwayne told him about his life. He told him about cars and school and television. But Andoo never wanted to leave the rain forest.

Dwayne loved the rain forest, but the ways of his own world were pulling him. More and more he found himself spending time in the city. He wanted a car. That meant he had to get a job. He came to the rain forest less frequently and when he did, he found Andoo changed. Andoo talked about having a wife. Dwayne had many more years of school ahead of him. He couldn't imagine being married. Andoo talked about his duty to his people. He asked Dwayne to join him. Dwayne was tempted. He would always love the rain forest, but he knew he belonged in another world. It was time for the boys to say good-bye.

Dwayne didn't go back to his rain forest for many years. He moved away from his parents' home and lived with some friends. One day he decided to visit Andoo. He returned to the back yard. The tent was gone. Dwayne's parents told him they had taken it down to build a deck. Some of the tropical plants decorated the deck, but otherwise there was no evidence of Andoo or his paradise.

Dwayne knew that somewhere Andoo still lived in their rain forest. He also knew he had made a choice to live another kind of life. In many ways he regretted his choice, especially when he realized that he would never again return. But in other ways he knew that he did not belong in Andoo's world.

32. To protect his plants as winter approached, Dwayne

    A   bought enough plants to make a rain forest.

    B   protected them with a plastic tent.

    C   brought birds and monkeys into the forest.

    D   brought the plants and trees inside.

33. The following diagram compares Dwayne and Andoo. On the left are facts about Dwayne. On the right are facts about Andoo. In the center are details that apply to both of them.

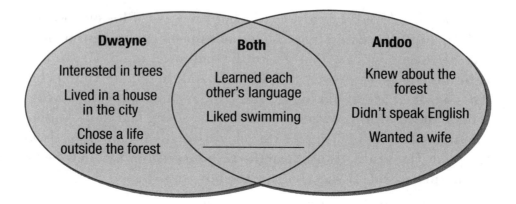

What belongs in the empty space?

A   told each other about their worlds

B   wanted to own cars

C   felt responsible for their people

D   built plastic tent

34. In this story, what does *specific* mean?

A   particular or unique

B   an ocean

C   an environmental issue

D   something very important

35. A good title for this story would be

A   *A City Boy*

B   *Swimming by the Waterfall*

C   *The New Car*

D   *Two Worlds*

36. What do you think would happen if Dwayne had been able to return to the rain forest and see Andoo?

   A   He would have stayed in the rain forest forever.

   B   He would have visited but then left the rain forest.

   C   He would have brought Andoo into his world.

   D   He would have decided not to visit Andoo at all.

37. When he realized he could never return, Dwayne probably felt

   A   happy that he had chosen to live in the city.

   B   angry with his parents because they had built the deck.

   C   sad that he would never see Andoo or the paradise again.

   D   afraid that Andoo was unhappy.

38. How do we know that this story couldn't have happened? Use details from the story to support your answer.

   _____

   _____

   _____

   _____

   _____

   _____